An Apple
for My Teacher

An Apple for My Teacher

Twelve Writers Tell About Teachers
Who Made All the Difference

edited by
Louis D. Rubin, Jr.

Algonquin Books of Chapel Hill
1990

published by
Algonquin Books of Chapel Hill
Post Office Box 2225
Chapel Hill, North Carolina 27515-2225

a division of
Workman Publishing Company, Inc.
708 Broadway
New York, New York 10003

Library of Congress Cataloging-in-Publication Data

An apple for my teacher : twelve writers tell about teachers who made
all the difference / edited by Louis D. Rubin, Jr.
    p.   cm.
    Reprint. Originally published: Chapel Hill : Algonquin Books of
Chapel Hill, 1987.
    ISBN 0-912697-57-1: $10.95
    1. Teacher-student relationships—United States. 2. Teachers—United
States—Anecdotes. 3. Authors, American—20th century—Biography.
4. Authors, American—Education. I. Rubin, Louis Decimus, 1923–
LB1033.A66   1990
371.1'00973—dc20   90-31845
                                                                 CIP

10   9   8   7   6   5   4   3   2

This book is dedicated
by its editor
to John Ernest Gibbs
and to the memory of Maurice Edward McLaughlin
who in their time made
the High School of Charleston
into what all schools should aspire to be
but so few schools can become.

Contents

viii   Contents

List of Illustrations

Preface

My notion is that most good writers are not born, but evoked. If you question them closely enough, you will usually find that for each of them there was an occasion, back when they were quite young, when the future author declared in effect that "a writer is a good thing to be, so I am going to be a writer." By no means was the decision inevitable; the writer-to-be might just as appropriately have elected to be an attorney, or a minister, or perhaps even a psychoanalyst. The reason that he or she chose to become a writer was that in each instance there was somebody who made him or her see that the literary life—ideas, knowing things, the putting together of words—was a dignified and worthwhile activity, meriting honor and respect. Usually that somebody was a school teacher.

I do not mean that the future writer did not already possess an aptitude for writing, or had failed to demonstrate incipient literary talent before encountering the teacher. Certainly no one can be taught how to write; if the necessary ability is there, one can be taught how to write well, but no more than that. Given the talent, given the innate inclination, however, it is possible for the right teacher to happen along and make the student heed the inclination and perfect the talent. Customarily this occurs in grammar or high school, though sometimes not until college.

Does this seem obvious? It is not really obvious at all. If the right teacher doesn't show up, the aptitude for writing may not be developed, or may be directed into other activities and result in other kinds of careers. The right teacher can be crucial.

I think, for example, of three renowned literary scholars, all of whom were students at the same small public high school in the town of Darlington, South Carolina, in the 1930s. Darlington was a small town, and in no way strikingly different from other such towns in South Carolina or elsewhere. What made these three persons decide upon literary careers was the presence at that high school of a particular Latin teacher. No one can convince me that if that teacher had not happened to be there, those three distinguished scholars would all have ended up doing what they do for a living.

At about the same time I was a student at the High School of Charleston, also in South Carolina. There was an English teacher, John E. Gibbs, Jr., and a Latin teacher, Maurice McLaughlin, on the faculty. They were very different kinds of people, but between the two they managed to point an astonishingly large number of youths in the direction of writing, literature, and scholarship. Throughout the four years I was there, from 1936 to 1940, Maurice McLaughlin never had more than seven or eight pupils in any of his advanced Latin classes; yet I can think of a half-dozen of his students during that time who have pursued careers in literature. John Gibbs also taught most of them, and was in addition adviser to the school newspaper (and if you were ever so careless as to spell it advisor, woe betide you); he turned out a number of professional journalists.

How did teachers such as John Gibbs and Maurice McLaughlin do it? It wasn't necessarily by making their students into accomplished Latinists, or literature scholars, or journalists on the spot. John Gibbs knew relatively little about journalism. And in my instance I was so inadequate a Latinist that in the first term of my senior year I pulled down an F and was able to graduate the following June only by virtue of having switched to a course in Business English for the final term. What they did, and what the kind of teacher I refer to did and no doubt still does, was to make their pupils view the acquisition of knowledge, the use of language, the professing of learning in general, as an eminently desirable and thoroughly respectable way to spend one's life. *What they* taught their pupils wasn't nearly so important as that *they* taught it—for if *they* considered it worthwhile to know things and be learned, as by their presence there in the classroom they so obviously did consider, then clearly those must be reputable and meritorious objectives for a young person to pursue.

From the worthiness of knowing and learning to the desirability of writing was an easy step; for isn't writing not only emblematic of knowing, but in itself an act of knowing?

Eudora Welty, in *One Writer's Beginnings*, tells of the formidable Miss Duling, principal of Jefferson Davis Grammar School in Jackson, Mississippi: "Her standards were very high and of course inflexible, her authority was total; why *wouldn't* this carry with it a brass bell that could be heard ringing for a block in all directions?" And she adds, "Miss Duling, in some fictional shape or form, has stridden into a larger part of my work than I realized until now."

Yet that can carry liabilities, too. For just as the Miss Dulings and the other teachers of future writers live on so admirably and lastingly in the books of their one-time pupils, so also do those long-ago teachers who failed to measure up, who through their example taught arrogance, cruelty, hidebound thinking, and even fatuousness, find their memorial in what their students reproduce in their writings. Unforgettable is the portrait of that Dr. Kennedy of Shrewsbury School, whom Samuel Butler depicted in *The Way Of All Flesh* as Dr. Skinner of Roughborough Grammar School. In Butler's warning words, "Never see a wretched little heavy-eyed mite sitting on the edge of a chair against your study wall without saying to yourselves, 'Perhaps this boy is he who, if I am not careful, will some day tell the world what manner of man I was.'"

This book is about the teachers of writers, as remembered by those writers. Each of the authors taking part was asked to produce a sketch of one or more of their teachers. No stipulation was made as to choice, other than that the teacher or teachers portrayed must have in one way or the other decisively influenced the writer. By no means are they all literature or writing teachers. George Garrett, for example, has elected to portray a pair of athletic coaches. Sylvia Wilkinson chose to tell of a science teacher. Fred Chappell writes of a fellow student. And John Barth tells of a student who became a teacher.

Mostly the portraits are affectionate, though not always. But all the subjects who sat for these sketches are, insofar as language can image experience, made very real, and, again insofar as words can stand against time, enduring. The reader will find comparatively little about the specifics of teaching in the sketches that follow, but a great deal about the art of being a teacher.

Today as always, when books about businessmen and politicians and sports figures crowd the best-seller lists, it is good to have this presentation of certain distinguished men and women, most of them unknown to the general public, who gladly learned and gladly taught for their livelihoods. Each sketch, I think, is by definition a specimen of the excellence they sought and evoked. To paraphrase the words carved upon Sir Christopher Wren's St. Paul's Cathedral, If you would see their monument, reader, read on.

Louis D. Rubin, Jr.

An Apple
for My Teacher

Elizabeth Spencer

Miss Jennie and Miss Willie

In a small town that's been there for ages, some people look out and some look in. (I look back, myself, quite a lot.) I now can see that the in-lookers far outnumbered the out-lookers. Back then, though, I wasn't given to that kind of seeing: I mainly just looked around me.

Photographs of those days powerfully back up my memories. From my birthday in late July onwards, the sun became so dominant there was no way even to think about it. Grass parched, people squinted at the camera, everybody under twenty, it seems, went barefoot. This was before air-conditioning. Houses could offer wide hallways with doorways front and back, and some had breezeways, others screened porches, good for keeping out bugs (if not all mosquitoes), nice for naps, and a necessity for sleeping at night.

As children, we played incessantly—in trees, in the creek, on the tennis court. We sometimes must have talked about what those late summer days were moving toward, sure and steady as the sluggish drift of the creek.

The schoolhouse was a two-story red brick building with cement steps up the front, set on a wide campus with swings and sliding-boards to one side, basketball courts to the other. It was right up the street from our house, scarcely a five-minute walk.

Once there, you had Miss Jennie. She was Mrs. McBride, really, a widow, but was always called "Miss Jennie." As everybody, young and old, had always had her as their first teacher through grade three, she drew a large part of the tremulous awe out of entering the new state of being. She

1

Elizabeth Spencer, age 9

was gentle, firm and quick, with eyes that twinkled at you from behind round glasses with black wire rims. Her hair, black and gray, was drawn back in a knot. Being happy to be with children, she was often smiling. She wrote a large, clear hand, dealt with ruled tablets and different colored crayons and blackboards. Penmanship, numbers, the alphabet, with letters large and small. Next, reading aloud, memorizing, multiplying. Three grades in one room. How did she manage? She and God would know the answer, certainly not I. We sang. Everything was all right in our Father's house (pointing upward), and it was joy, joy, joy (circling hands) over there.

We came into the room (quietly, if you please) while she stood at the open door. We marched out in files, following a small flag. Mounting upstairs to chapel once a week, we

Mrs. Jennie Nelson McBride

Carrollton, Mississippi, High School, 1930s

would go in rows carefully stairstepped by height, and all the older grades laughed as we paraded to our seats. Down in our classroom we also marched in and out for recesses, and raised hands for "being excused."

Discipline? Stand in the corner with your face to the wall; write "I am sorry" ten times on the blackboard; stay in after school; or, coming up to the front, have your hand bent back, palm up, and get five slaps with a ruler. That last is the only one I remember catching; it didn't hurt the hand like it hurt the pride. I sat through arithmetic trying not to cry.

Miss Jennie taught us the alphabet by Bible verses: "*A* good name is rather to be chosen . . . ," "*Be* ye kind one to another . . . ," "*Create* in me a clean heart . . ." Asked for Bible verses in other groups, some of the smart boys used regularly to quote, "Jesus wept." Miss Jennie was ready for that one. Not even when we got to J did we get to say "Jesus wept." Her verse began with Jesus, all right, but was longer. So on through the alphabet.

Everybody's parents approved of Miss Jennie; every child respected Miss Jennie; Miss Jennie was beloved. Faced with her greatest test, a woman who wanted a crazy, obstreperous child to learn with the rest, she let the child in, gave her a seat and tied her to it. I used to see her writhing out of the corner of my eye. She once ran berserk and pushed me down on a brick walkway, cutting my lip. Miss Jennie sent upstairs for my brother to take me home, bleeding and bawling. I still have the scar.

Retired from teaching, Miss Jennie lived quietly in her house up near the Presbyterian Church, where she regularly taught the little children in Sunday School, right on to the end. She let out rooms, I understand, to difficult old ladies who must have been worse than any first- or second- or third-grader, but could not be enjoined to stand in a corner, much less smacked with a ruler. A new primary school building was named, of course, for her; there was never any way for Carrollton, Mississippi, ever to let her go. There was no way to think of Carrollton without her. Even to let go of her at the end of the third grade was bad enough. I got scared all over, during July and August. The only cold spot in the world was at the pit of my stomach. No longer to know precisely one's place in line, to get "Well done" for saying the memorized verse, to write correctly the names of Columbus's three ships, to march behind the little flag.

Who would teach us next? It was a real question because the depression had struck and the school (I remember many worried conversations when my father returned from meetings of the school board) had hardly the money to operate.

During my last year in Miss Jennie's room, two new students entered late in the year. They had been living somewhere else. They were sisters named Meade Marian ("Mimi") and Frances Keenan. Mimi was always laughing, while Frances, quieter, had a good many thoughts of her own. They wore their little dresses much shorter than we were allowed to do, rather like little paperdoll children, skirts flaring up to the lace on their panties. In winter, when my mother would sometimes walk up to meet me after school, she would see them and say, "I don't see why those children's legs aren't freezing." Maybe they were. Their air said that style was more important than discomfort. They knew what they were doing. The Keenan girls.

Late in August of that year we heard that the school had employed their mother, Mrs. Keenan, to teach grades four and five. "Lucky to get her," was my mother's judgment. "All that family is smart and Willie especially." She had come back from somewhere else to live there; her husband, a man no one seemed to know much about, was employed elsewhere.

She was a member of a leading Carrollton family; her grandfather, or so I recall, had been a U.S. Senator, and others of a bright, decidedly alert disposition could be met among us or heard about from elsewhere. One of her cousins, Mr. John M——, drove cows back and forth to pasture for his wife, Miss Annie, but if you stopped to speak to him, it was politics, current affairs, or history he'd read you a lesson on. All that sort of thing was going on in his mind (though not neglecting the cattle). He let his hair grow long and never went to church.

I first saw my new teacher on a street uptown, walking on one of those sidewalks which, due to erosion and road-scraping, had got much higher through the years than the roadbed. I was riding in the family car. It was August—hot, blazing. She had on a bright blue dress with a flounce, almost to her ankles, and her long hair was caught up in a careless "bird's nest" way, puffed out over the brow. All this looked interesting. She walked with her head down, rapidly, the flounce swinging. "There goes Willie Keenan," my mother said. "I bet she's burning up in that dress."

In early September we got our new books from the druggist who always kept them. On the appointed day we entered our new room with caution, took seats and waited. She had arranged her desk. No playthings, cut-outs, colored stars or maps. Books. And a few flowers. The hair was the same as I'd seen. The voice was nothing we were used to. It came from other places. For one thing, speaking to any one girl, it said "darling." We never used that word. Full of endearments—"Honey," "Sweetheart," "Precious," "Baby," "Sugar," even "Sugarfoot"—we had read "Darling," maybe heard it in the picture show, but didn't say it. Mrs. Keenan did.

She was wearing glasses: horn-rimmed, they slid down to the tip of her nose and stayed there. Her hair, rich brown laced with gray, frothed over her brow. I think now she must have been pretty in a taken-for-granted way. She tapped the books. We would use them when we could, she said, but she had no use for very much that was in them. (Astounding rejection.) "Take literature, for instance," she went on. She paused. I must have heard that word before, but didn't remember where. We had lots of books at home. We were always reading, or being read to. But I don't remember hearing it called "literature" before. She said she had ordered another book for us. It would come.

Mrs. Kay Keenan

From then on, awakened somehow by the words she had used, the sense of her return from far-off places, the climb up from young school to real school, the difference in her little girls' dresses (one was now across the aisle from me), I could not wait for that book. Never had a Sears, Roebuck order been so fervently expected. I remember it still. It was a narrow, tall volume, bound in pink paper: *One Hundred and One Best Poems*. It may be (I don't know) that she was never trained as a teacher. Laws about degrees in education came later. Mrs. Keenan would correct our arithmetic, give a passing hour to grammar and geography, but what she really liked was reading poetry. After lunch-hour recess was over, she saw us through some routine chore before she would open the pink book and read. I guess the poems were way over our heads. There were Shelley's "Ode to a Skylark," and "Ode to the West Wind," Kipling's "Recessional" and "Gunga Din," "Abou Ben Adam" (I think she skipped that one), Browning's "Incident at a French Camp," and "How They Brought Good News from Aix to Ghent," also MacCauley's "Horatius at the Bridge," even some Edgar Guest (skipped also). One began "I saw the spires of Oxford/As I was passing by/ The cold grey spires of Oxford/ Against a cold grey sky." This troubled me as I had been once or twice to Oxford, Mississippi, and knew there were not any spires there to speak of, certainly not cold gray ones. There were softer poems like "Annabel Lee," and "To Helen" by Poe, and Sidney Lanier's "Song of the Chattahoochie." She would explain things to us about these poems. Some odd phrases would have to be spelled out. "A kingdom by the sea," was not a real place, only where the poet imagined it, though he might have been, it was true, near the ocean. Then why couldn't it be a kingdom? Maybe it was, darling. There was also "Thanatopsis" by William Cullen Bryant. I couldn't make head nor tail of it when I first read it, but I had a cousin, older than I, who knew and quoted poetry, though he went to a larger school in another town. He would fill in if I started something. When I piped up that

I'd read the one about "So live that when thy summons comes
. . . ," he went right on with "to join that innumerable cara-
van that leads to that mysterious realm where each shall take
his chamber . . ." I finally caught on. It was dying that was
meant. "Approach thy grave," etc. Until then, the sound of
the words, the stately march of the rhythm were all I knew.

Each of these poems had a short preface of a few lines about
the author, and a picture in a small oval of the poet's face.
Tennyson had whiskers, Shelley looked scared, Byron wore
a white collar, Poe had funny eyes, Elizabeth Barrett Browning a fancy hairdo. Mrs. Keenan (or "Miss Willie" as some of
us dared to call her) liked to read us "The Bells" by Poe. When
she read it, swaying from side to side, repeating "bells, bells,
bells, bells, bells, bells, bells," hairpins used to fall out of the
nest above and scatter over the desk. She didn't notice. Neither did I. I used to feel uplifted, absorbed, not in that room
at all.

She assigned us themes and let us write our own poems.
This for me was easier than learning to swim or climb a tree.
It continued and amplified my trance over the poems. The
pink book, getting worn, was never far away. I had had stories read me constantly, since I could understand, but no one,
I think, had read poems aloud to me before. Certainly not
like that. Somebody in the family at home happened to remark that Rudyard Kipling had died. I took the news sorrow-
fully to Miss Willie. "Nonsense," she said. "He couldn't die
without my hearing it." She was right. What world was this
of hers, where you heard at once that Kipling had died? I
turned in themes and poems.

It was still fall the first time she came down to talk to my
mother. I knew she was coming, and I was naturally excited.
It was an afternoon in November, after school. I sat down
with them, minding my manners and not saying anything—
listening to grown-ups was my specialty—when I was suddenly asked to leave the room. I understood at once that she
meant to talk about me. I think I tried to eavesdrop, but failed.

I went out back and talked to old Bill, our handyman. When I returned she was gone and my mother had a complex look on her face. I still don't know if she was glad of that visit or not. She had probably been completely happy with Miss Jennie. I later learned that I was to be thought of as "talented," "imaginative," etc.—all those superlatives Miss Willie had to give, and all the backing her old family name could bring to bear on them. To me, her opinion, right or wrong, simply flowed out from the poetry, "the bells, bells, bells." It joined me more than ever to the poems, and along with them, to Miss Willie and that outer world she came from, saying "literature," and "darling," and knowing when writers died.

At a students' program in the evening before school let out that spring, I was asked to read a story I had written. Miss Willie read it for me, as I was too timid, and the cry of the small town audience was for "Author, author." I got up to be applauded, but what I felt about this, and the reason I couldn't read my story aloud, was by now a solitary thing, which frightened me because it was powerful and could not be shared. It had already separated me from my school friends, and I became for a time an outcast, ostracized and mocked at, my blue tam stolen, my books and homework hidden, the road to school and back a miserable trek among cold mud puddles.

I was reading the pink book alone in the living room one day when my brother, seven years older, came in. He asked what I was doing. I told him just to listen and began to read aloud. He seized the book, tore it from my hands, and began to read the poem in a high voice, leaping around. When I reached for the book he hurled it across the room and danced out, waving his arms in some kind of triumph.

My father was worried about money. My mother, I think, was worried about me. In the summer, I kept writing stories. I used to go to secluded places among the woods and bluffs that were part of our property, ride my pony down to the creek, lock notebooks away in my room. One hears of the

Elizabeth Spencer—*Piboska Mihalka*

joyous discovery of new worlds, but to me this is glib. There is no denying that my new-found ways were causing me miseries of loneliness, pangs of feeling "different," evasiveness, and secret anxieties. I showed things I had written to my mother and sometimes to one of my jollier uncles, but it would be many years before I found any real community, or even knew that such a thing existed.

The Keenans moved away. Perhaps Mr. Keenan sent for them. Their going was not a real surprise, and I don't remember it as painful. Mimi and Frances had sometimes come down to my house to play. I think I always understood that they belonged to the somewhere else they had come from, were among those few who looked outward. Yet even those who go away have ties they don't lose: the day the request came for me to write about some teacher—"some particular teacher who got you impressed with literature and writing"—I received a letter from California from someone I'd never heard of. Who was "Kay Keenan"? It was Miss Willie. This letter was the first I remember getting, though she'd left our little town in the early 1930s, as I recall. Miss Willie, now eighty-nine years old, now known as "Kay." She enclosed the last letter she had had from my mother, who died in 1974. Evidently they had kept in touch, my mother as fixed in place as Miss Jennie; Miss Willie, the wandering one, outward bound. Sure enough, she was leaving California for Virginia, and hoping I would write.

Teachers that came my way after her were wonders, who will remain with me always: Virginia Peacock, in high school, who, like Miss Willie, put aside the school texts for welcome detours through *Romeo and Juliet, Julius Caesar,* and *The Merchant of Venice,* with dalliance also over Hawthorne and Dickens; J. Moody McDill at Belhaven, who showed us so many horizons and kept me writing at a time I wanted to stop; and Donald Davidson at Vanderbilt, that famous character, who made me see modern literature for the first time. But I still think it was Miss Willie who let it all in on me. From then on there was a working out—a working outward, toward a world of which she was mysteriously but naturally a part. Back then, I mentioned once to my mother that Miss Willie had said the story of Adam and Eve in the Bible was "just a story." (She had actually said this rather casually, not in the manner of teaching anything or imparting some startling truth.) My mother, however, was terribly alarmed and told my father, who took a grave view of it. "With that kind of talk," one of them said, "she's leading those children astray." I guess she did.

Fred Chappell

Welcome to High Culture

When we think how many people it takes to produce one writer—how many tolerant relatives, gracious teachers, forbearing friends, and imposable strangers—it becomes obvious that the end product is not worth all the effort. But then, what is? It takes just as much warmly disinterested effort to turn out an athlete or a scientist or a responsible citizen. The State is going to spend the money anyway, those merry folk who have patience with young people are still going to be amenable; so that we may consider the appearance of a poet or fiction writer as an unexpected bonus, as the civilized world always has done.

Usually, though, the first serious encouragement that greets a writer is well-intentioned discouragement. "Writing," said my high school teachers, "is a good hobby, something you'll always be able to do. But don't expect to be successful at it. Most aspiring authors never get published." My parents saw the prospect in an even gloomier light, or darkness, than my teachers. Most of my friends thought I was certifiable for the mental wards, or was striving to become so.

It makes no difference. If a writer is going to write, he writes; if he does not write, then he is no writer. I didn't know what I was supposed to do with the first poems I wrote at ages twelve, thirteen, and fourteen. I buried many of them in the bottom cornfield, returning them to the soil I felt had given them birth. Others I placed on wood chips and, after setting them afire, floated them along the turgid currents of Duckett's Creek. I watched them drift out of sight, feeling jubilant and forlorn at the same time . . . Such grandiose self-pity neither helped nor harmed the feverish lines on the Blue Horse notebook paper.

But—thank you, Mrs. Kellett. Though you never lodged the fourth declension in my disordered head, you showed me that others besides myself could be excited by books. I haven't forgotten the story of your becoming so absorbed in Dickens by lamplight that the room filled with smoke and you never noticed.

Thank you, Bill Anderson and Fuzz Fincher. It was good to have high school friends who thought that I was only immensely silly and not raving lunatic.

Thank you, Tom Covington, wherever you are, whatever course of life you pursue. I never learned to write a proper science fiction story suitable for those magazines, but you did manage to teach me to write a straightforward sentence, a comprehensible paragraph. I can still recall my astonishment when you broke off our correspondence upon joining the Navy; I had pictured you as a wise old man, in his thirties *at least*.

Once having opened the Catalogue of Debt, writers, even the most regretful and bitter among us, could go on and on and on, like the tearful young ladies in the Academy Awards ceremonies, until our audience too would cry out, "Say, didn't you do *anything* yourself?"

And that question ought to be taken seriously. Writing is such an inescapable part of literate culture, such an ordinary part of communal aspiration, that a writer should not much pride himself on his precious volumes. Even if he is the most radical of thinkers, someone who desires to tear his culture down and build it again from the bottom up, society—American society, anyhow—can turn to him and say, "Yes, but the reason you were educated was to enable you to think precisely these thoughts." The radical writer in America is stuck with this anomaly, that his only audience is the literate Establishment, who are by and large a broadminded and tolerant bunch. This fact makes him fight the band that heeds him.

Because one of the guildmark characteristics of a young writer is self-dramatization, it may be that many of the early slurs and snickerings he endures are partly imaginary. A writer seems to feel instinctively that it is necessary to have something to struggle against, and I have met no writer, even among best-selling novelists, who did not believe that this reviewer or that one was out to get him, that his publisher has not advertised him lavishly enough, that his agent is an economic simpleton. This attitude of aggrieved affront may be a holdover from the years when none of the heartbreakingly pretty cheerleaders sufficiently adored his sonnets. Or it may come down to the other fact that writing is an inevitable part of culture, that a writer owes too much to too many, that at last he does have little for which he can take personal credit, and all this makes him uneasy and defensive. For no matter how many Miltons, Chekhovs, and Prousts have appeared or shall appear, the writer in the end remains what he was in the year 6000 B.C.—the village scrivener, a clerk.

Perhaps the cruel world is aware of this fact, perhaps that is why it gives him such a hard time. The village vests a heavy responsibility in its scrivener, who is to draw its portrait, preserve its memories, and keep its accounts, both material and spiritual. Perhaps the world is careful to weed out those not nervy enough to do justice to the office. If the writer prefers to impute motives of heartless jealousy, that is only more instance of his trying to make himself look good to himself.

But then he has to look good to himself, since to everyone else he looks merely odd.

College! I thought. If I can ever graduate from high school and get into college, I'll find kindred spirits, other people who will sympathize with my aspirations and respect my goals. I had heard of the legendary teacher of creative writing at Duke University, Dr. William Blackburn (though I thought his name was "Blackstone"), and I was confident that I was the student he had been praying to come along. I had given up science fiction and had recently written two heavily symbolic stories that were so mythically sophisticated I couldn't understand them. I was just hell on symbolism, and I felt certain that Dr. Blackstone would appreciate these superior endeavors.

I got into Duke all right, though it is not clear how I did— not on the strength of my high school grades, surely. There I found out that freshmen were not allowed into the writing class. I would have to get through my first year, making passing grades in my physics and logic classes, before I was eligible to be admitted to the sanctified novitiate. And then I would have to submit a manuscript that met favorably his iron scrutiny.

A year, that year, it seemed to me, would be ten eternities coupled together like boxcars. I would shrivel and die, scarab beetles would gnaw my dessicated bones tangled on the chair and writing desk of my dormitory room, before that year passed. What in the world was I to do in the meantime?

I drank a great deal of beer and whiskey, and I wasn't very expert at it.

And there was a literary magazine, *The Archive*, which was the oldest college literary magazine in the United States, and had, among my convivial unliterary buddies, the reputation of being the dullest publication the Lord ever suffered to plummet from the presses. "Dull, is it?" says I. "*Archive*, your nondescript days are past. Here comes Fred Genius with his stories and poems to set you zooming the glittery avenue to international acclaim."

Then another obstacle presented itself. *The Archive*, I found out, had an editor. If the editor liked your material, he published it; if he didn't publish it, he returned it with a note explaining why it was unspeakable garbage. This editor's name was Reynolds Price. He was a straight-A senior, and he was, by all accounts, nobody's fool. Other undergraduates spoke of him with contempt, of course—in the way they spoke of all the literary crowd—but with *awed* contempt.

The most interesting revelation was that he was a flesh-

and-blood human being like anyone else one might run into on campus. My experience with editors was that they were sinister spectral entities who occasionally scribbled crabbed notes on little blue rejection slips: "Your exposition is silly"; "This is not how Martians talk to each other"; "The pace of this story is like a Boy Scout hike—half trotting, half dawdling." But Reynolds Price was a student like myself . . . Well, no, he certainly wasn't that; but he did live in a room on the third floor of the Independent Dormitory. My first obvious step toward making *The Archive* a famous magazine would be to accost this man and flash my blinding credentials.

I got cold feet. What if I wasn't such hot stuff as I'd been telling my shaving mirror? What if I was an ignorant hayseed from a farm three miles outside of Canton, North Carolina? What if Reynolds Price decided to talk in French? What if— what if, after all—what, O God, if I wrote badly?

I had already made friends with the deeply pondering, slow-talking poet James Applewhite, and I confided my plan and my fears to him, delighted to discover that he had considered the same plan and had nursed the same fears. We decided to pool our courage and face the wizard together.

The pool of courage we resorted to was an unwise quantity of beer and cooking sherry. Our evening of destiny started early and got late quickly, but when we felt we had girded ourselves sufficiently, we returned to campus and stumbled up the narrow stairs. We pounded, lurching, on his door and Reynolds let us in.

Into, it seemed, an entirely different universe. Our rooms in the freshman dormitories suddenly seemed a thousand miles away, those rooms with the mimeograph-paper-green walls and bare, pocked linoleum tile floors and for decoration only the naked, inscrutable smiles of Hugh Hefner's pinup girls. Reynolds' room was another kind of place. It was agreeably lit with lamps, not with those bald overhead lights found in dormitories and police stations. There was a rug on the floor; it wasn't large or expensive-looking, but it meant that

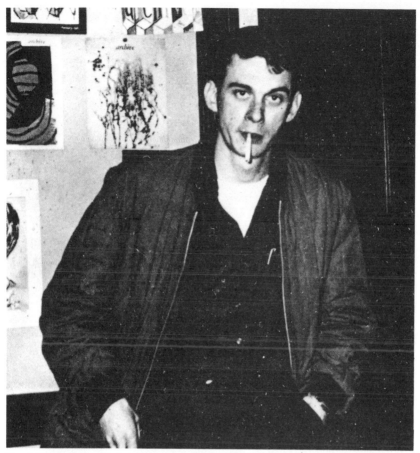

Fred Chappell as Duke University student—*Duke University Archives*

Reynolds Price, 1952

we didn't feel we were hiking a chopblock when we crossed the room. On the walls were *framed* reproductions of Botticelli and Blake and Matisse, on his desk a miniature of a classical torso. A record was playing—Elisabeth Schwarzkopf, I think—and there was an autographed photo of her on the wall.

"Hello, jerks. Welcome to High Culture," Reynolds said.

—No, he didn't. He couldn't say those words, or think them in an eon of trying. Yet I had the fleeting but certain conviction that he was entitled to say them.

In fact, he was polite and cordial, much more so than the situation warranted. Reynolds has almost always managed to maintain a smooth and pleasant demeanor to match his pleasing looks, and I hope that his easy manners have always worked as sturdily in his service as they did during that awkward evening. He treated us amiably, with a reserved humorous gravity, no doubt having sized up our unsober conditions. We sat—that is, we collapsed into chairs—and he sat, and we attempted conversation.

Reynolds talked then just as he does now: fluently, nonchalantly, knowingly, allusively, and always with a partly hidden humor. His manner was so assured that we began to question the impulses that had brought us here, and our defensiveness returned to bully us worse than before. Jim and I began to pretend to talk more to each other than to our host, dropping scraps of poetry and code names, *Pound, Eliot, Hart Crane, Rimbaud*. The friendship of young writers is usually marked by this cryptic patter; it is as if they feel themselves members of a spy ring. But Reynolds picked up our hints.

The horribly deflating thing was that he not only picked them up, he bandied them easily, as if these subjects which had cost Jim and me so much trouble to find out about were the common and legitimate coin of social intercourse. That was a blow. There are always writers or certain kinds of writing that other, especially young, writers feel proprietary about, and I have watched even famous poets and novelists

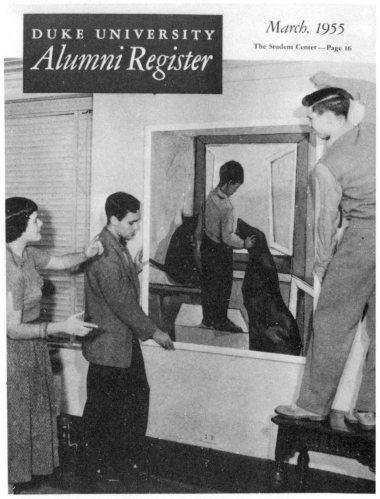

Cover of Duke University *Alumni Register*, March 1955.
Reynolds Price is holding painting—*Duke University Archives*

turn mildly belligerent when someone else in the room evinced knowledge of works which they have decided belong, godammit, only to them. But here was Reynolds Price, cheerfully, blithely, opining right and left in territory where Jim and I felt we had, if not first claim, then squatters' rights, at least. He made it worse by being invulnerable; it was clear he had actually read the stuff he talked about.

That fact ought finally to have made us furious, but it didn't. Reynolds' insouciance began to work a calmness upon us, and we began to relax a little, to enjoy ourselves. We began to welcome the discovery that here was someone else who was *one of us*. It got to be time, and long past time, for us to depart, and there was little pleasure in walking back through the mazy halls to the freshman dormitories. My position in life seemed grubbier to me than ever before, and I made stiff resolutions to change myself.

I could not change my life and it later brought me to minor disaster and major embarrassment. But that was not Reynolds' fault; he did the best he could with me, and it is astonishing to me now that a young man of twenty or twenty-one could have so much cheerful patience with a prickly adolescent only a few years his junior. There is a patience which is born of experience, but there must also be a patience born of innate wisdom, and it is this latter that Reynolds was graced with.

I began to bring him my work to read, long arcane poems and wild confused stories. I have mercifully forgotten this material by now, and almost all that I remember is Reynolds' good-natured meticulous attention as he went with a pinpoint-sharp pencil over line and line, word and word. His queries and objections on the page were delicate little breathings of graphite. This is how Rilke must have read through manuscripts, I would have thought—if I'd known who Rilke was. Sometimes he would use technical terms to criticize rhythms and tropes and I would never admit that I didn't know what those terms meant. "Ah yes," I said, nodding. "I

James Applewhite—*Duke University Archives*

see." Thinking, What in the name of seven sunken hells is an amphibrach?

He must have admired my persistence, at least. There was one longish, heavily Eliotic, tainted poem that I brought to him some dozens of times. Was it about a mystic nun? I can dimly recall only some image about a stained glass window. I must have written that poem forty times, following his intimations and encouragements. It never worked out. Finally I wrote an ugly parody of it, then gave up. And there were many other pieces to which we gave the same treatment. I spoke loudly and quarrelsomely in their favor; he argued gently and reasonably against certain passages. Little by little I would mollify and acquiesce at last.

He was never wrong. He wasn't always right; he was sometimes unable to diagnose the *exact* illness of a passage, and he would sometimes object to certain phrases and subject matter out of inevitable and necessary personal prejudice. But he was never wrong; his objections made logical, if not always artistic, good sense; or they appealed to some separate standard I'd never heard about or to some authority unknown to me. (Who, pray tell, was Herbert Read? Who was Geoffrey Scott?) It didn't matter whether he was right or not; it was too important that he was never wrong.

I learned a great deal, perhaps as much about literature as I ever learned from anyone. I trudged to the dictionary and looked up *amphibrach*, to the library and checked out Read and Scott. Mostly I picked up knowledge simply by contact, the way the cat in the weedy field picks up beggar's-lice and Spanish needles. I learned that even the pantheon contemporary writers were living sinful creatures like me and the postman. Reynolds possessed a kind of movie-fan worship of writers and loved to collect gossip about Auden, Faulkner, Welty, Hemingway, and he loved to pass it on. These tidbits must have been special fun to pass on to a wooly kid who would sit openmouthed to hear about William Empson's toping habits.

He published a couple of his own stories in *The Archive*. They were good stories, appearing later in his collection, *The Names and Faces of Heroes*. Strange that they did not influence my fiction, because I certainly admired their accomplishment. But maybe it was already clear to me that Reynolds and I were headed in different directions. There seemed to be a tacit agreement that I was to be intense and wild and experimental, while he was to be traditional, Olympian, and successful.

Everyone who knew him took his eventual success for granted, and "eventual" was assumed to be only a few short years off—as indeed it was. Reynolds took a Rhodes scholarship, as we all knew he would, and impressed the powerful literary figures at Oxford, just as we expected him to do. "A Chain of Love," the longish story he wrote for Dr. Blackburn's class, Stephen Spender published in *Encounter*. Reynolds then returned to Duke as a freshman composition instructor and wrote his first novel. *A Long and Happy Life* was published to lucky, but well-deserved, wide acclaim. Here was his picture in *Time* and on the cover of *Saturday Review*. His carefully planned career seemed to have flourished exactly on schedule, and this fact occasioned some inescapable natural resentment, even from me. Maybe especially from me.

There were some gruff times between us at this period, but in the end they didn't matter. My gratitude was larger than, though perhaps for a while not as fierce as, my jealousy. I never forgot what I owed to Reynolds, and if I ever do I shall have become someone the human race ought to cease speaking to. Sometimes I've wondered if others have remarked the Goethean qualities about the man, his steady adherence to the highest ideals, his immense easy knowledge of all the civilized arts, his cultivated ease. It is an index to his character that if he reads these present lines, he will not be embarrassed, however much he may disagree with what they say.

There were others besides Jim and me for whom he was mentor. There was the poet Wallace Kaufman and the novelist Anne Tyler, and there must be many others of whom I am

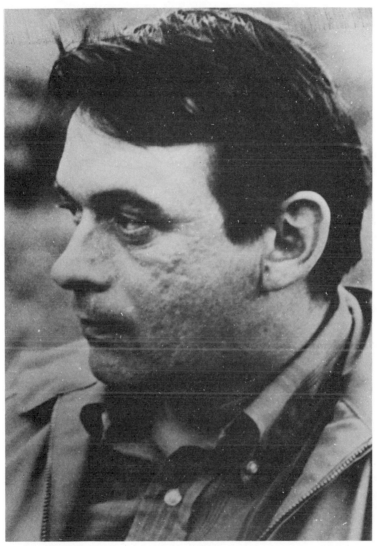

Fred Chappell—*Duke University Archives*

unaware. Their memories of Reynolds will differ vastly from mine, and yet I can't help imagining that their essential experiences of him as friend and teacher must be like mine in general outline.

He was, you see, a genuinely cultured person, and there are precious few of them in any situation, even in the universities. If you happen to entertain the fantasy, as I once did, that these figures are to be met with only in novels or history books, then you will be pleasantly shocked to meet one as a friend. It marks us when we do; it refreshes our ambitions and reillumines our sensibilities; it warms, for a longer time than we expect, our cooling existences.

In order to conclude in proper fashion this excursion into heartfelt sentimental nostalgia, it has occurred to me that I ought to drink a glass of wine in honor of Reynolds Price. What is needed is a rich red, full-bodied wine, with an earthy but not harsh aftertaste, a rather soft finish. There is no drink like that in the house and I shall have to go to the wine shop, describe to the proprietor what I'm looking for, and ask his advice.

That is the difference between us, of course. Reynolds would know the correct vintage and the best year.

Alfred Kazin

Teachers—and
Two Particular Teachers

I n 1931, sixteen years old, I became a freshman at the College of the City of New York. "City College" was in upper Manhattan, an hour and more on the subway from my home in Brooklyn, but the newly established Brooklyn College did not attract me; too many of my high school classmates were going there. I was looking for new people as well as some older collegiate tradition. Brooklyn College was impromptu, raw, making do in office buildings around Borough Hall. It was so new that a friend of mine had written the school song, which defiantly began, "Though these are not towers of marble . . ."

City College was famous, awesome, severe. It had been founded in 1847 as the "Free Academy" and boasted such distinguished alumni and ex-students as General Goethals, who had built the Panama Canal, Upton Sinclair, Bernard Baruch, Felix Frankfurter, Lewis Mumford, and the philosopher Morris Raphael Cohen, who in my time was the most celebrated member of the faculty.

Thousands of the city's schoolteachers were graduates of City College. To the native-born children of immigrant Jewish families (which most of its students were) and especially to the families themselves, City College had a mystique, a reputation for scholarly achievement and intellectual seriousness. I, like most of my classmates, had been incessantly pushed all my young life to be a scholastic over-achiever. To this day I can remember my fear of "school," my fear of disappointing my parents in the all-important matter of school, and my sense of dread every Friday morning when I left for

Alfred Kazin, in 1930s

the weekly "tests," that I was incapable, guilty as hell, and would prove the ruin of all those people who so anxiously watched over me. On the other hand, my "success" in school was to help lift them out of the tenements that contained and stifled all our being.

I had no choice in the matter of college. My parents had never heard of Harvard. Such were the tight bonds enclosing poor Jewish families in those primitive days that I would have had to decline a scholarship "out of town" if anyone had (inconceivably) thought of offering me such a thing.

City College at 137th Street was at one end of the West Side I.R.T. subway line and my home in the Brownsville section of Brooklyn was at the other. But it was not altogether a hardship to travel the whole route twice a day. I could usually get a seat on the subway and read away to my heart's content before I exited at 137th Street to climb the long hill past Lewisohn Stadium to my classes in the imposing black-and-white checkered Gothic structures off Convent Avenue.

The campus featured a statue of the West Pointer, General Alexander Webb, attired in full uniform but lacking his sword, who had helped to found the original "Free Academy." His sword may have vanished long before my time, but his West Point emphasis on mathematics was still there to harass my days and nights; freshmen had to take a year of calculus. At the entrance to the Main Building was Gutzon Borglum's large head of Lincoln. Inside the Lincoln Corridor, the main hall, was a statue of George Washington and a large American flag. These presented themselves awesomely just outside the office of the dreaded registrar, Morton Gottschall. Gottschall was supposed to have been the perfect student in his time, all A's. He seemed affable enough, but such was my dread of falling behind in the battle for "good grades" that I thought of him as an obsessive clerk in one of Dickens's counting houses, constantly hunched over the vast ledgers that showed my grades. Nothing in this life would ever seem so important to us and our parents as those daily, weekly, monthly, semester-long indications of our progress.

The Lincoln Corridor was airy, spacious, lovely. In glass cases outside the faculty offices were displayed faculty publications and illustrations of the college's history. Even more pleasing to me was the Great Hall, with its famous mural lining the stage showing some worthy youth being initiated into the Valhalla of academic tradition. The flags of the world's great universities, beginning with the oldest in Europe, Padua and Salamanca, hung from church-like rafters. I often took refuge in the Great Hall, impressed by the show of tradition, which was in such contrast to my poverty and the political turbulence surrounding us in the 1930s. Since I was markedly a loner, who wanted to do nothing but read, I often secreted myself in the Great Hall. I liked the procession of university flags over my head and from time to time was lucky enough to catch the professor of music practicing Bach on the great organ.

Below stairs, in the "concourse," was an extraordinary circulating library, shelf on shelf in this densely layered humpbacked space, which was packed like some cavernous wine cellar. We had the free run of the library. Indiscriminate reading was a fetish. As Isaac Babel said in one of his marvelous stories about young Jews in Odessa before the Revolution, the first commandment was "You Must Know Everything." Of course a lot of showiness went with so much reading. The philosopher Morris Raphael Cohen, the most illustrious and most feared member of the family, was humbly watched every Friday afternoon to see what special morsels he took out for *his* weekend reading.

The concourse was divided into "alcoves," separate walled areas, each with its own benches and Ping Pong table. Over the years each alcove had achieved its identity as the particular headquarters for some (usually leftist) ideology. Each alcove was in bitter rivalry with the other alcoves. The years 1931 to 1935, my years at City College, saw the depths of the depression, a quarter of the labor force unemployed, the beginnings of Stalin's terror against his old comrades in the Bolshevik leadership. The children of Russian Jews had grown up on tales of Czarist oppression, pogroms, and so had intense interest in the original promise of the Russian Revolution. Strange as it may seem now, when so many of my once radical classmates have become "neo-conservative" (even the wealthy stockbrokers among them have never recovered from their disillusionment with the Revolution), the "alcoves" believed themselves on the brink of great events.

I felt myself engulfed, as I wrote in *Starting Out in the Thirties* (1965),

by Socialists who were Norman Thomas Socialists, old-line Social Democrats, Austro-Marxists; by Communists who were Stalinists, Trotskyites, Lovestoneites, Musteites, Fieldites; Zionists who were Progressive Labor Zionists, left Socialist Zionists. All the most accomplished philosophers ever born to the New York streets, tireless virtuosi who threw radical argument at each other morning noon and night with the same curves and smashes with which they played ping pong at each other in the college basement that smelled of the oily sandwiches that we brought from home—I was not worshipful of ideologists. Yet I believed in socialism, if not in the savage "proletarian" exclusiveness of the Communists . . .

Some of my classmates were to become Nobel laureates— the physicist Robert Hofstadter, the biologist Arthur Kornberg. Of course I never met them. On my very first day at college I was impressed by the tall blond figure of Albert Wohlstetter, a future head of the Rand Corporation and "nuclear expert" who in those days was a radical program setter always surrounded, to my envious eyes, by disciples. The actor Zero Mostel (first name adopted in token of the tyranny of school over him) was another classmate, as wildly assertive and raucously funny as he was to be on the stage and in any restaurant where you happened to meet him thirty years later. Another was Bernard Malamud, but he was so quiet that I never got to know him until long after we had left college.

It was the faculty, and especially those Jews from the student ranks who had unbelievably made it into the ranks of the faculty, who dazzled us constantly. The leading professors in the English department had such acceptable names as Mott, Horne, Otis, Palmer, Compton, Stair, Tynan, Roberts, Johnson. Professor William Bradley Otis was a charmingly humorous but definitely not serious man, with an antic public manner which did me more good than his instruction in American literature. He liked to tell the story of how he had gained his appointment to the faculty. Apparently in those days knowing someone big in Tammany Hall helped considerably. "Your name is William Bradley Otis, *Bradley* the second name? You're hired!" College president Frederick B. Robinson, who like the English department head Lewis Freeman Mott still wore a cutaway and a Vandyke beard, had occasion one famous afternoon to call us "guttersnipes."

By contrast with affable Bill Otis, the philosopher Morris Raphael Cohen, despite his Harvard Ph.D., had been permanently soured by having to teach mathematics for many years as a mere instructor. He longed for the graduate students he would have had in a great university and was profoundly disagreeable with the likes of us. Cohen was aggressively sharp in his famous logic course, specializing in what *he* called the "Socratic method," which was often merciless interrogation of a student; Cohen would easily dispose of us. When asked by one crestfallen student "What do you leave us with?" Cohen triumphantly replied "What did Hercules leave when he cleaned out the Augean stables?"

I valued Cohen's teaching because he put us onto Santayana's five-volume *Life Of Reason*, a textbook in his main philosophy course. I disliked him and the showy rationalism he offered as a solution to all life's problems. It was not until I had left college that I learned how different he could be with friends and the many professional philosophers he had trained—Sidney Hook, Paul Weiss, Ernest Nagel, Milton Munitz.

I majored in history as well as in literature, and was stupefied by the young Edward Rosen, an alumnus, who had begun his life work, his epochal translations and annotations of Copernicus's Latin treatises. It was typical of City College, of a certain time and place, of a traditional Jewish intellectual, that Ed Rosen, engaged all his life in a study of Copernicus's heavens, should have presented the appearance of a gruff taxi driver. We were all rough characters; some of us were so because we were intellectuals possessed, intellectuals to our fingertips. Others were possessed by "making it," and still are. Teachers, prime authority figures, penetrated our lives, stamped them forever, as only our parents had done. They were in fact another set of parents, all the more vivid to us because, unlike so many parents, they spoke English.

I was led into writing, positively pushed into my lifework, this constant need to write, because teacher after teacher did not know what to make of me. I was a stammerer (like my mother), an embarrassment and hindrance in class. But I felt boundlessly free when I sat down to write anything in the private notebooks I started keeping as a boy. This project became a description of street life and city life based on my passion for walking the city, for looking beyond the tribal life of my neighborhood. Like my father, whose poignant idea of freedom was to keep walking, to look for an exit, I found in walking a prime literary resource, a basis in observation.

In the Franklin K. Lane High School, two teachers inadvertently, and with no particular awareness of what Camus called "a special case," got me writing. Samuel Zisowitz—Samuel Martin as he later became—was an enthusiastic reader in class of Sinclair Lewis's "Young Man Axelrod" and Theodore Dreiser's "The Lost Phoebe." These two stories, sentimental as they seem now, certainly not their authors' best work, gave me lasting images of the Middle West as great American country—the "valley of democracy," the old rural life. Dreiser in particular presented gnarled, deep qualities of feeling that made him a special favorite of mine. Long before Dreiser was accepted as the great if ungainly writer he was, I fought to do him justice. When my first book, *On Native*

Grounds, was published in 1942, Dreiser was so amazed by my admiring chapter on him that he sought (vainly) to make me and James T. Farrell alternate executors of his estate. Without Sam Zisowitz reading Dreiser to a high school class it might have taken me longer to incorporate *Sister Carrie* and *An American Tragedy* into my imagination.

A major inspiration in high school was a history teacher, Julian Aronson, who happened to be proctoring an examination I was taking. He changed my life by forbidding me to leave the room after I had handed in my papers long before the closing bell. When I asked him for something to read, he flung me some more yellow test paper and in his weary, ironic way said, "I suppose you can write? Write something!"

It was something about a violin. Like all good Jewish boys of my time and place I studied the violin. It was understood that I would become great and famous on the concert stage. Like Heifetz, Elman, Milstein, Horowitz, Rubenstein, I would take my parents with me into the great blue yonder. Aronson, observing me writing away, asked to read my sketch. He grinned; and still grinning, took me to lunch. That thin, weary, bitter grin grew more and more pronounced each day of that last week in high school. He lent me books by early Zionist sages, picture books by Marc Chagall, and leading me off to Highland Park for a walk around the wonderfully deserted reservoir on the border of Queens, listened to me read aloud from my early essays, poems, and sketches of city life.

It was 1931, the summer of my graduation from high school, the beginning of that cardinal summer when, day after day, wild with gratitude and surprise, I began to take in what I would live for. Aronson must have been a very young man then, not long out of the city college to which I in my turn would be going that fall. He was very offhand, forever drawling out sarcasms when he thought I needed taking down. He seemed to me very stoic and wise in that thin, weary way he had; he never paid a compliment to your face.

It was typical of his sardonic temper that he once noted (out of a corner of his mouth) that he had been lucky to have grown up in a grocery on the East Side. "There is always *some* money in the till." Every warm full June afternoon that last week of high school, I would wait for him (some new composition in hand) on Evergreen Avenue in the Bushwick district, staring and staring at the trees lining the quiet streets beautiful with gray frame houses and brownstones. We would walk past the German ice cream parlors and up Bushwick Avenue in that extraordinary summer's peace I associated with the sight of so many awnings lining the street, stop at his house to hear recordings by Kreisler and Casals, and at last, steadily mounting the hill that led into Highland Park past Trommer's brewery, go up to the reservoir through the cemetery. In one place a little Chinese group lay all by themselves.

By contrast City College was cold, bleak, an education factory. To major in literature, I was informed by one roughneck after another the week of registration, was "sissy." Only the sciences—especially chemistry, in which City College had a notable tradition—were virile enough for the likes of *us*. My first paper in freshman English was an oedipal piece about helping my mother carry ice back to our kitchen, each of us holding one end of a towel. This was such a familiar and happy experience for me in summer that I was astonished by the young instructor's disgust on reading my paper. He was a vaguely British type, a recent Oxford graduate (the University of Oxford was often on his lips) who openly disliked his predominantly Jewish students. My loving description of carrying ice in partnership with my mother seemed to him, as he tightly put it, "impossible to comprehend."

Another instructor in English, famous for his dry comments on anything that went beyond the boundaries of his *very* restrained temperament, noted of some effusion of mine, "Methinks you drive Pegasus too hard." The seventeenth century was just coming back then, thanks to Eliot. I was very happy indeed to discover Donne and Herbert in Donald Roberts's classes. Roberts was a large, melancholy man, long exhausted by the teaching grind habitual in those days—four courses a semester. He occasionally published a review in the *Nation,* which made him a literary star in the department. Edgar Johnson, the future biographer of Dickens and Scott, was a charming relief from theatrical types like Joseph Tynan, the specialist in drama, who was supposed to have been an Irish rebel escaped from the British police, and William Bradley Otis, who spent many of our class hours denouncing William Randolph Hearst, but who was intellectually so simple that it became a point of pride to read forbidden literature like Joyce behind the official textbook.

The presiding atmosphere at college was emphatically not literary but political. Everything turned on which local brand of salvation-by-Marxism you adhered to. Of course fascism was the great threat in those days, not communism. When it was announced that a delegation of "Italian Fascist students," as they were described, was touring American colleges and would appear among us, a violent demonstration against them took place in the Great Hall. My college career would have ended if I had not been sitting in the balcony studying Stephen McKenna's translation of Plotinus. The head of the student council, a bristling Stalinist who was to be killed in the Spanish Civil War, abused the visiting Italians to their faces as Fascist scum. One of the Italians made a futile effort to say something. (I learned many years later that the "Fascists" were mostly Jews and dissidents.) The militants in the hall shouted and moved toward the stage. The dean's staff took photographs of the melee, and students who could be identified making an uproar were summarily expelled—some twenty-two.

President Robinson had a near-altercation with protesting students on the campus. He waved his umbrella and denounced them as "guttersnipes." Many students wore lapel buttons reading "I am a guttersnipe." War between the student body and the administration became a holy cause for some of the more intransigent students. One of my favorite classmates, a Communist amusingly irreverent about The Cause (he defended Stalin's purges on the ground that when *he* became a Communist leader he would shoot Earl Browder and other such horrors), made a point of writing his papers in Greek Philosophy on the backs of leaflets.

It was a relief to escape into the classes of Bird Stair, the greatest teacher I have known and the man who more than any other led me to discover myself as a writer.

No one remembers Bird Stair except his now aging students. He was a Hoosier, otherwise without distinction, who presented a plain, blunt appearance. He was bald, solid-looking in expensive tweed suits, and seemed to grow hair everywhere except on top of his head. Tendrils of hair groped out of his nose and ears. Otherwise there is so little to say about his person, and I actually know so little about him, that I can remember every "witty" remark he made. One, whose relevance to my own situation was mysterious, was the orphic warning: "Remember, Alfred, the hardest way to earn money is to marry it." Although he had never completed his Ph.D., he allowed himself to be called "Doctor" by one of the many apple polishers in the student body. He said to me with a self-appreciating smile, "I've taught for so many years that I deserve the title."

And that was Bird Stair, whom in our irreverence (he was a formidable figure behind his desk) we called "Birds, Beasts And Flowers?" Not quite. Unlike most of the senior professors, Stair knew his stuff. Sometime in 1934 or 1935, when Henry James "had been dead for some time" (T. S. Eliot), Stair amazingly made us read the great man and even more amazingly told us where to find his books. This was long before the paperback revolution. James was by no means widely accessible in those days, especially not to students who could not afford the New York edition and had not known that first editions of James at depression prices could still be picked up in the bookstores that lined Fourth Avenue.

Even as he brought James to our attention, Professor Stair lacked charm. He tended to hammer away; he made a point of being brusque. His hard, metallic Midwestern directness echoed in the classroom like a farmer shouting at cattle. His comments at the end of a student paper, even when they were approving, invariably shook me. His handwriting was harshly angular, each letter strenuously precise. His authority in the classroom was bullying. But unlike the famous Morris Raphael Cohen, whose mastery of the "Socratic method" was designed to expose the student's ignorance, Stair strove to bring students up to his own level of literary consciousness. And this was what he accomplished in my case, although his many years of teaching had hammered him into a kind of chisel.

Stair taught the writing of criticism, using for his textbook the little Oxford World Classics volume of *English Critical Essays, Twentieth Century,* edited by Phyllis M. Jones. It is before me as I write. There are essays by old stagers like George Saintsbury, W. P. Ker, Robert Bridges. The final essay, and one that had the greatest possible influence on my understanding of modernism, was Virginia Woolf's "Modern Fiction," from the first series of *The Common Reader.* This early defense of James Joyce made me understand the intoxication with the "stream of consciousness" that was to become the essence of high modernism.

Life is not a series of gig lamps symmetrically arranged; life is a luminous halo, a semi-transparent envelope surrounding us from the beginning of consciousness to the end. Is it not the task of the novelist to convey this varying, this unknown and uncircumscribed spirit, whatever aberration or complexity it may display, with as little mixture of the alien and external as possible?

Virginia Woolf began her essay with a criticism of Bennett, Galsworthy, and Wells as "materialists."

In contrast with those whom we have called materialists, Mr. Joyce is spiritual; he is concerned at all costs to reveal the flickerings of that innermost flame which flashes its message through the brain, and in order to preserve it he disregards with complete courage whatever seems to him adventitious, whether it be probability, or coherence, or any other of those signposts which for generations have served to support the imagination of a reader when called upon to imagine what he can neither touch nor see.

After that epochal and revolutionary praise of Joyce (for 1933), Woolf went on, just as significantly, to say that for all his originality in *A Portrait of the Artist as a Young Man* and our first glimpses of *Ulysses,* Joyce was less satisfying than Conrad in *Youth* and Hardy in *The Mayor Of Casterbridge.* I have never forgotten the emphasis which Bird Stair put on the following passage in the Woolf essay. The cemetery scene in *Ulysses,* Woolf said,

with its sudden lightning flashes of significance, does undoubtedly come so close to the quick of the mind that, on a first reading at any rate, it is difficult not to acclaim a masterpiece. If we want life itself, here surely we have it. Indeed, we find ourselves fumbling rather awkwardly if we try to say what else we wish, and for what reason a work of such originality yet fails to compare . . . with *Youth* or *The Mayor Of Casterbridge.*

It fails because of the comparative poverty of the writer's mind, we might say simply, and have done with it. But it is possible to press a little further and wonder whether we may not refer our sense of being in a bright yet narrow room, confined and shut in, rather than enlarged and set free, to some limitation imposed by the method as well as by the power? Is it the method that inhibits the creative power? Is it due to the method that we feel neither jovial nor magnanimous, but centered in a self which, in spite of its tremor of susceptibility, never embraces or creates what is outside itself and beyond?

Thanks to Bird Stair—and Virginia Woolf—I was led into the very heart of the modernist revolution, and at the same time made aware that the famous stream of consciousness can be made stagnant by the quality of *mind* that portrays itself in that stream.

What Bird Stair did for my reading was wonderful. What he did for my writing was—everything. The last paper I did

Alfred Kazin—*Martha Kaplan; Alfred A. Knopf*

before graduating was an appreciation of the drama Brahms liked to work up in his stormy music. Music has always been a special passion of mine; I was an uncertain but determined violinist, and so addicted to my favorite performers that I took odd jobs in order to be near Carnegie Hall on great nights. I remember nothing of the paper I did on Brahms; it must have been cloyingly rhapsodic in the over-appreciative fashion that marked me in my young days, when life seemed to consist in daily discoveries of something new and wonderful in art.

In any event, there came a day, an unforgettable day, when Bird Stair returned my Brahms paper to me with the dry comment: "You have a talent for this sort of thing. I should pursue it." Stair's terse clipped approval woke me up. I began doing literary reviews for the *New Republic* when I was still in college, wrote regularly for a variety of magazines after my graduation, and was full of my own writing when I was briefly a graduate student at Columbia.

Mark Van Doren was at the height of his career at Columbia. No one could have been less like Bird Stair while duplicating Stair's magical effect. So far as I know, Stair never published a line. Mark Van Doren was one of the writing Van Dorens; his elder brother Carl accurately called Mark "the most gifted of us all." He was noble, he *looked* noble: craggy, humorous, beneficent, wise. He was poet, novelist, editor, film critic for the *Nation;* his doctoral thesis at Columbia, *The Poetry of John Dryden,* had been acclaimed by T. S. Eliot in a famous essay sparking the Dryden revival.

At the same time Mark Van Doren was a passionate admirer of Thoreau, a superb anthologist of world poetry. In his famous course on "The Long Poem" he was such a spellbinder that after almost half a century I can still remember the extraordinary figure he presented. I described in *New York Jew* (1978) Van Doren's

peculiar spare look of nobility, that grave deep voice that made me think of Emerson declaiming sonorous periods in his famous platform voice and a habit of eloquence that had made Van Doren the

Mark Van Doren—*Columbia University*

perfect teacher of a winter afternoon in Philosophy Hall. After his lectures on Virgil-Dante-Milton we followed him home to Bleecker Street on the Seventh Avenue Local so as to continue a conversation that ranged from Homer to Hart Crane.

Mark Van Doren was a great American presence. The word was central to his teaching and being; the historic Van Doren voice hugged the words, saying them in love for some old America. You could never forget that the Van Dorens came from Hope, Illinois. One of his most beautiful poems had the line,

Six great horses of Spain, set free after his death by De Soto's men, ran West and restored to America the wild race lost there some thousands of years ago.

Ironic to contrast the two greatest teacher-influences on me—Bird Stair and Mark Van Doren. One was entirely ungifted, except in the classroom; Van Doren was a spellbinder without effort, a magnetic presence, because he was so gifted everywhere else.

In any event, thanks to you all, teachers dread and teachers dear, thank you all! I am what you have made me. God alone may be able to forgive you.

Elizabeth Forsythe Hailey

A Fellow Conspirator

M y mother first pointed her out to me in church, returning to her seat from the communion rail. Her face
radiated a serenity I suspected came from an intimacy with
God that I, a shy and awkward adolescent memorizing cate-
chism in preparation for my confirmation, was still struggling
to achieve.

"That's Siddie Joe Johnson," my mother said. "The writer."

I was awestruck at the thought that a real writer was sitting
just a few pews away, confessing her sins and praying for
absolution like the rest of us.

From earliest childhood, characters in books had been as
real and vivid to me as the people and animals I saw every
day. I loved Muffin, the dog with the cinder in his eye in
Margaret Wise Brown's wonderful "Noisy" books, as dearly
as my own black cocker spaniel, and it was Lucy Fitch Per-
kins' twin books that gave me my first sense of countries beyond my own, along with the reassuring notion that though
the children might be different on the outside, on the inside
they were very much like me.

However, as much as I loved books and as close as I felt to
the characters who lived in them, I had never expected to
meet an author face to face. Authors, I imagined, were special
people who lived separate, private existences in exotic places.
But here was a writer living in the same city I did—Dallas,
Texas—and attending the same church—St. Matthew's Episcopal Cathedral.

At the coffee hour after the service my parents introduced
me to this ethereal creature who to my amazement was

Elizabeth Forsythe Hailey, age 12, right

laughing and chatting and eating doughnuts like everybody else. My mother mentioned that I liked writing stories and poems and plays for my sisters and me to perform.

"Do you want to be a writer?" she asked kindly.

"Yes," I whispered, overwhelmed by the audacity of my response. I liked writing stories but "to be a writer" was an ambition I had never dared admit, even to myself, let alone to anyone else.

The next thing I knew she was inviting me to join a creative writing class she taught one afternoon a week at the downtown public library where she was children's librarian. At once flattered and terrified, I accepted.

The following week, armed with a brand new spiral note-

Old Dallas Public Library—*Dallas Morning News*

book labeled "creative writing," I took a bus from Stephen J. Hay Elementary School, where I attended the sixth grade, downtown to the main public library.

Traveling alone by bus made this class different from the ballet or horseback riding or tennis or diving or art classes to which my mother endlessly chauffeured my sisters and me— part of her master plan for making us into well-rounded people. I had no particular interest or aptitude in any of those fields; the classes were my mother's idea and, for lack of any urgent or even interesting alternative, I took them to please her.

But the invitation to attend the creative writing class had been extended to me personally by a real writer, who I dared hope recognized in me similar stirrings if not yet proven talent. And this time my mother was not driving—I was traveling alone, on a city bus.

Dallas in 1950 was a different place than it is today—as was any city in 1950. "Everything's nifty in nineteen-fifty," I remember my Sunday School teacher greeting me on New Year's Day—and indeed it was. I live in Los Angeles now and I cannot imagine allowing, let alone encouraging, my daughters to take a bus anywhere by themselves. And yet I am saddened to think they are missing the exhilarating sense of independence I felt traveling downtown on a bus full of strangers on the first step of my journey to become a writer.

It was with an enormous sense of importance that I entered the imposing building where the central library was housed. The suburban branch library near our house was a regular stop on my mother's weekly circuit, between the laundromat and the grocery store. My sisters and I, dressed in our Saturday blue jeans or shorts and sandals, would roam the stacks, looking for storybooks to while away the long afternoons. But this was my first time inside the downtown library. It had the feeling of a shrine. I was glad I had worn my best sweater set and new saddle oxfords. It seemed appropriate somehow that having first encountered Siddie Joe Johnson in church, I would find her ensconced during the week in a secular temple devoted to books.

I arrived early that first day and spent the time before class looking in the card catalogue under "J," marveling at how many cards were lined up behind the name Siddie Joe Johnson. I remember thinking that having a card with my name in the library would be as close to immortality as I cared to come. I still feel that way. Whenever I visit a new town, I love going to the local library and finding my name in the card catalogue (or, more recently, on microfilm, but a name on the screen is far less satisfying than a card you can hold in your hand).

I went to the shelves and took down one of the children's books Miss Johnson had written—*New Town in Texas*. Leafing through the pages, I saw that it was about a girl my age, living seventy-five years earlier but otherwise not so different. I was amazed that an important author like Siddie Joe Johnson would find the adventures of a twelve-year-old girl worth

Siddie Joe Johnson—*Dallas Public Library*

writing about. I decided to check out the book and take it home with me.

I approached the round table where the class was gathering very cautiously. Writing was something I'd always done alone in my room. I wasn't sure how I felt about sharing my poems and stories with strangers. But the dozen or so students around the table didn't seem much older or more experienced than I was. It was the first time I'd taken part in anything involving students from other schools that was not a competition of some kind. I began to relax once I realized we were in this thing called writing together.

Miss Johnson—who, I soon learned, liked to be called Miss J.—sat among us, a fellow conspirator rather than a judge presiding from a desk at the front of the classroom like every other teacher I'd known. She began the class by reading a story aloud. I was embarrassed at first. My mother had read me bedtime stories when I was little but no one had read aloud to me since I'd learned to decipher words for myself. However, I'd never heard anyone read a story the way Siddie Joe Johnson did—like a sorcerer casting a spell.

She was not a beautiful woman by conventional standards. Her grey hair was parted in the center and pulled straight back on each side. Her distinctively arched eyebrows emphasized the piercing eyes which were her most striking feature. They stared at you through curving, cat-eyed glasses, appraising everything, taking nothing for granted.

At first glance this was a severe woman, plainly dressed, very little jewelry, sensible shoes. And yet she used makeup subtly and skillfully to emphasize her high cheekbones and dramatic features, and when she spoke, it was not in the stern, authoritarian tones of a schoolteacher but in the warm, rich, seductive voice of an accomplished courtesan. As I listened to her read, features that at first seemed forbidding became almost glamorous in my eyes.

She was not a frustrated actress—she never attempted to act out the story nor did she accompany the narrative with gestures or emotional outbursts. She simply read the words in a quiet, clear voice, allowing their inherent mystery and power to work in the imagination of her listeners.

After the story she read a poem—John Masefield's "Sea Fever." I can still hear the rise and fall of her voice bringing the crash of waves and the sting of salt spray into that landlocked room. Most of us had never seen an ocean, but Miss J. had grown up in Corpus Christi on the Gulf of Mexico. It was clear as she read the poem that she was reliving her own experience as a young girl.

Then it was our turn. "Now who has brought something to share with the class?" she asked expectantly. The boy sitting next to me raised his hand. "I want to get this over with," he said apologetically then plunged into a poem about a boy who'd broken his leg playing baseball, sliding home for a tie-breaking run. I knew before I saw the crutches under the table that he was writing about himself—and I remember feeling uncomfortable at how much he was revealing. It didn't even sound like poetry—full of slang and awkward rhymes.

When he finished, I waited nervously to hear what Miss J. would say. I hoped she wouldn't be too hard on him. It was clear to me he was only taking the class because he couldn't play baseball. But to my amazement she applauded and said he'd made the best possible use of poetry—to transform experience. "How'd you really break your leg?" she then asked with a smile. He blushed and mumbled something about tripping over a hoe in the back yard. She assured him it was all right and said you didn't have to be true to facts when you wrote a story or poem, you just had to be true to your own feelings.

I was glad he'd gone first because the next person to read convinced me I was in the presence of a professional. She was a tall, thin girl with intricate French braids that I couldn't help studying as I listened to her recite. Her rhyme scheme was as complicated as her hairdo. I was sure Miss J. would offer to send the poem straight off to her own publisher, and it would be printed in a book. What was I doing in that class?

"I think you must have liked that poem by Wordsworth we read last week very much," Miss J. began, oh so gently. Then she went over the parallels between the two poems, never accusing the girl of anything but trying to imitate something she admired. No one ever left one of Miss J.'s classes feeling like a failure.

The next week on the way to class I met Miss J. outside the library. As we crossed the street, the wind whipping our coats about our legs, she turned to me and said with a smile, as if we were speaking our own special language, "This wind's like a whetted knife." I was astonished to hear that phrase from the poem she had read the week before translated into something I could feel on my skin. At that moment I began to see the possibility of poetry in my own experience. Perhaps sensing I was at a turning point, Miss J. began the class that day with her own definitions of poetry: "Poetry is washing dishes   and hoping you will see a rainbow in the suds. Poetry is seeing the whole sky in a single drop of dew. Poetry is what happens every day to everybody."

Thrilled by the discovery that my own life was worth writing about, I turned everything I did into a poem and fearlessly read my new work each week to the class. I was so enraptured by the sound of my own thoughts, I stopped paying attention to the other students and what they were writing. I do remember that the boy with the broken leg stopped coming to class once it healed. Poetry proved no substitute for the playing field. Once he left, I was writing for only one person—Miss J. I cannot imagine a more sympathetic audience. She listened as if each one of us was a poet laureate. Occasionally she might suggest a better word or a different approach, but she never embarrassed anyone with her criticism.

When I look back now at the poems I wrote that year, I marvel at her tolerance. ("I love to picnic in the park. I play and play until it's dark." Could she really have listened to that with a straight face?) Yet from the beginning she treated me, treated all of us, as her equals. I began the class thinking of her as a famous author. By the time of her death in 1977 at the age of seventy-one, she had published two books of adult poetry and ten books for children, including *Feather in my Hand*, *A Month of Christmases*, and *Cat Hotel* (which, I'm told, she submitted originally under the title "Cat House," quite innocent of another meaning). But it is as a sympathetic friend that I remember her now.

After class each week I would walk the few blocks from the library to the bank building where my father had his law office. While he packed his briefcase for home, he would allow me to use his dictaphone to record my new poems.

Listening to Miss J. read aloud to us each week, I had begun to understand that words were living entities, whose shape and sound were as important as their meaning. Indeed during that year I was seduced more than once by the sound of a word at the expense of its meaning. I still remember sitting in my father's desk chair, dictaphone in hand, recording what I thought was the most important poem I had ever written, a patriotic ode that went:

> Flag of America,
> May you always be
> Symbol of truth
> And iniquity.

What I do not remember is anyone correcting me. Could I have recorded that poem without first reading it to the class? Had I grown so blindly confident of my own ability in so short a time?

I am not sure how many weeks or months I attended the class, but it was long enough to convince me that the words I put on paper were more than just another way of amusing myself on a rainy day, like the pictures I painted or the figures I shaped out of clay. I began to see that writing was a serious business, something as valid and important as the work my father did all day in his law office. I loved driving home with

Elizabeth Forsythe Hailey—*Kendall Hailey; Delacorte Press*

him from downtown after class, knowing my mother would be putting dinner on the table and preparing to listen as we recited our day's accomplishments. I resolved then that whatever else I did with my life, I would not be one of those wives who waits for her husband to bring her news of the world.

Growing up in Texas at that time, I knew very few professional women beyond my father's secretary, my doctor's nurse, my teachers at school. Siddie Joe Johnson was like none of these. She was a woman with a higher calling who supported herself, both literally and spiritually, through her imagination. For her, books provided not just a source of amusement but a livelihood. From hence forward, I was prepared to follow her example, to travel by bus or train or plane, alone if need be, earning my own living with words.

For Christmas that year, instead of buying a present for my parents as I usually did, I copied out my poems, bound them with cardboard, tied them with ribbon—and dared believe they were a gift worth giving.

John Eisenhower

Misterfoglesir

My first recollection of the man who was to become the most influential teacher in my life centers on an inauspicious incident. The incident was trivial, I admit. But it set the stage.

Time: a pleasant Saturday afternoon, early 1937. Place: Brent, a small coeducational boarding school in the mountains of Northern Luzon, Philippine Islands. Background: Jack Cook and I, two high school freshmen, banging a Ping Pong ball across the net upstairs in the boys' dorm.

Jack and I were well-matched, as I recall, but I was ahead, about to close in for the kill. (We were, I admit, making a lot of noise.)

Suddenly a door on the mezzanine below burst open. A lithe figure, clad only in underwear, straight black hair every which way, sprang up the dozen steps. The message was out before the figure halted at the Ping Pong table: "You two cease that racket; I'm trying to sleep!"

Cook and I stood there agape. I mistook a moment of silence for uncertainty. Tentative, I asked, "Question, sir?"

"What is it?"

"Can we just finish the game?"

"No!" he roared, forgetting Cook and turning on me. Then, he caught himself and added, rather sourly, "That's the weirdest thing I ever heard of."

Misterfoglesir gave a last stern glare, turned on his heel, and bounced much more slowly down the steps and into his room. The Ping Pong game was over, no doubt about that, but we giggled slightly. We had gone to the brink of disaster,

John Eisenhower at Brent School

peeked over the side, and had come back chastised but feeling secure. As a youngster raised in the Army, this was something I could understand. Clear-cut lines of authority, obedience, and (above all) no hard feelings afterward. For we knew that "Old Deadpan" would never mention the incident again, probably never think of it, unless to chuckle. He was too sure of his own rightness ever to apologize for his outburst. But then he would never hold my mild impertinence against me, either.

That incident could never, in itself, explain why this tall, spare, rather dour English teacher could be the idol of the boys at Brent (and maybe some of the girls, too). I have to look beyond that. Maybe it was that very sense of his own rightness that appealed to us—we would like to be sure of ourselves some day as Mr. Fogle was sure of himself now. Maybe it was because he was not only the school basketball coach but head and shoulders a better player than any of the youngsters on his team, despite the fact that some of them were approaching twenty and he was an antiquated twenty-four.

Yes, that was it: he was simply the best athlete in school.

Faculty and students of Brent School, Luzon, 1937. Richard Harter Fogle is seated, left, first row; Catherine Cox, seated sixth from right; John Eisenhower is standing, fourth row, fifth from left, next to column.

Before I had ever set foot on the basketball court a couple of months before, I had asked if we had a coach. "Do we have a coach!?" was the reply. "You ought to see him!"

Well, see him I did. Poorly coordinated though I was, the school was small enough that all members of the student body were required to try out for the basketball teams, boys and girls. On the court, Richard Fogle was like a cat—quick, graceful, intense. Yes, intense. Maybe I should say "tiger" rather than mere "cat." For his intensity flashed from his black eyes even when simply demonstrating a run-up dribble shot. Though his job was coach, he taught basketball the only way he knew how. He played it with us, sweat-band soaked around his forehead, shouting terse commands, disciple of the fast break. He hadn't been captain of the Hamilton College basketball team for nothing.

Off the basketball court, Mr. Fogle presented an entirely different figure, almost humorous compared to the tiger on the court. He walked as if his feet hurt. Come to think of it, he had been that way the day of the Ping Pong game: he had sprung up the steps as if on the basketball court but had tripped back down as if his feet hurt.

But even with that minor idiosyncrasy Old Deadpan was the model of dignity. His presence commanded everyone. There was nothing pompous about him. Though he did indeed "bestride the narrow world like a colossus," he did so quietly. The fact is, that dignity I just mentioned tied in with the hurting feet; he took every step as if he were just exactly where he was supposed to be. He was. Books in arms, usually wearing the little wire reading glasses that added fifteen years to his age, he was right where he ought to be, aloof, hardly seeing, but in the right place. He appeared seven feet tall, though I'm sure he was less than six feet. He unobtrusively and unconsciously overshadowed our congenial, brilliant, but slightly pompous headmaster—though perhaps that was in my eyes only.

But I'm supposed to be telling about a teacher, not a figure.

Richard Harter Fogle, 1937

Brent School basketball team, 1937. Coach Fogle is seated, top row, left.

In the classroom Mr. Fogle exhibited his third personality, the independent thinker. Here he soberly considered every piece of work we studied, be it an essay, "The Paradox of Poverty in the Midst of Plenty" (that's where I learned the word "paradox"); Ben Franklin's *Autobiography;* the works of P. G. Wodehouse; Holmes' "The Last Leaf." I could name more; I couldn't do that for any other class I've ever taken. Fogle examined each one as if it were a bug in his magnifying glass. He listened to our opinions with respect, as if we had some sense. He made pithy, memorable comments about works, comments that I know were not in printed texts, for they were too independent.

Thus Ben Franklin, he observed, had written this autobiography before he had done anything we would remember him for. But then Old Ben would later justify his former self-importance. P. G. Wodehouse, especially *Jeeves*, was fun for him and us. But Wodehouse himself, as history proved later, was "weird."

And the tiger of the basketball court was gentle in the classroom with unprepared students who tried to bluff. What if I did try to argue that Mandalay was in India? Kipling wrote "The Road to Mandalay," didn't he? And Kipling wrote about India, didn't he? Aha! And what if Kipling did mention a Burma girl in "The Road to Mandalay"? I overlooked her, and she was probably selling Burma-Shave anyway. But Professor Fogle did not accuse or condemn; he merely corrected. Mandalay *is* up the Irrawaddy River in Burma, isn't it?

Mr. Fogle was nobody's Mr. Chips. No pipe and tweeds, no bull sessions in his small, austere room. But in that small school, only fifty students in all the high school, a family atmosphere pervaded. And in the gatherings out by the front fence or wherever, Mr. Fogle carried forward the same respect for each individual that restrained him from putting us down when we were obviously off-base in class. We didn't exactly take our meager troubles to him, but I, for one, tended to act a bit outrageously at times to attract his attention. Thus in

freshman year, before puberty was complete, I adopted a pos-
ture as a "woman hater." How I expressed that pose I don't
remember. But I do remember Fogle's chuckling and saying
casually, "Jack, some day you'll realize that there are two
sexes and they have to get along." Nothing more—and he
was the only person who ever called me "Jack." Even that
minor exchange gave me a feeling that I may have been mis-
led but certainly was not just a wet-nosed kid.

Back to the academics. For some reason I have always
tended to associate Richard Fogle with the English language
itself. A slightly narrow view, considering that there have
been other masters of the tongue such as Shakespeare. I wonder why, but I have a theory. Just as Fogle looked like he was
in just the right place when walking to the dining hall, he
acted as if he was in just the right place discussing Oliver
Wendell Holmes. Our discussing Oliver Wendell Holmes was
the most important event going on in the world—or at least
the Philippines. In this Mr. Fogle was gifted by a deep sten-
torian voice and his deliberate manner. He liked to read
aloud, and when he did, every word was understandable, it
sounded important. If Old Deadpan, our hero, believed in
this—if English was that important to *him*—then even irreverent youngsters must conclude that a study of the English
language must be all right.

But Richard Harter Fogle had his vulnerable side also. I
think he was bored at first during that year of 1936–37, per-
forming his duties conscientiously but with a great deal held
in reserve. That is, until he began to notice Miss Cox, the
comely and demure grade-school teacher from somewhere in
the Deep South. Miss Catherine Cox was always the model
of decorum. She kept to herself, aloof from the gossips of the
faculty, and always presented a bright, pleasant face to the
world. After a while it became noticeable to our fourteen-
year-old eyes and ears that Mr. Fogle had a way of sort of
sidling up to wherever Miss Cox happened to be in a group.
Gone was the self-assurance; gone was the boredom. In their

places was uncertainty. The tiger/colossus/professor was now an awkward guy, one hand in pocket, silly sort of grin, trying in vain to appear casual and suave. Silently we cheered him on, hoping that Mr. Fogle and Miss Cox would somehow "get together." They did at the end of the next year, summer of 1938, leaving for home and marriage. We all applauded.

Commencement, 1938, didn't mean much to me. I was a sophomore, going to be a junior the next year. Hardly a cause for a big celebration. But as soon as the ritual was over, I had something on my mind, something I had to do. I climbed the steps to the mezzanine in the boys' dorm and knocked on Mr. Fogle's door. "Come in," he called. He looked up quizzically from his packing. "What's up, Jack?"

I eased in. "Mr. Fogle," I choked out. "I—I wanted to wait until all the grades were in and all that. But I wanted to say, we're sure going to miss you around here."

The quizzical look softened. "Jack," he said evenly, "I hope I'll see you in the States some time."

"Yes, sir." I was out the door and that was that. The States were a long ways away and we had our own paths to follow.

The story ends happily. At a Brent reunion a couple of years ago, only a few faculty members appeared, but among them were Richard and Catherine Fogle, married forty-five years, parents and grandparents. They were the centers of attention. He was now University Distinguished Professor of English, emeritus, Chapel Hill, North Carolina, and a world-renowned Hawthorne scholar. She was no longer just handsome; she was radiant. It was good to pick up again after so many years.

And in our too infrequent visits, I learned something startling. Those eyes of his that had seemed to stare off into space and notice nothing, noticed just about everything. And Miss Cox, detached as she had seemed, had also been taking in everything that had gone on. I know now, because we have reminisced at some length.

We are now in our sixties and seventies (but who's count-

John Eisenhower

ing?). The great leveler of age has removed former barriers. But not quite. I'm glad that Mr. Fogle has adopted the dignified nickname of "Rich" rather than the more intimate "Dick." After all, we still can't get too familiar with the Quiet Colossus of Brent.

Max Steele

English 23a: A Paper Long Overdue

As it will every Thursday afternoon that fall semester of 1942, rain is slanting against the gray stucco sides of Main Building, making blotted animals that race under the wide Florentine eaves and through the sparse ivy near the top of the Bell Tower. It is a beautiful building with that calm suggested by any building, picture or story whose proportions are just. It is noble without being pretentious and makes one think of Italy but not of the War, even though a ministerial student standing in the library doorway is saying: "The War, that's why we're having all this rain. All that bombing. My daddy says it rained every day during his basic training in World War I." And since the past is as unknown as the future, who can dispute this wisdom?

The bell in the tower clicks twice as it always does before the first toll. Now full tones roll out through arches and over the sashay of rain on the library roof. Car doors open and slam and from them, last minute students run across the soggy lawn, under the baring gingko trees, and over the slippery leaves which gild the sidewalks.

Inside, in a first floor room which connects the old wing with the new, Advanced Composition, English 23a, is meeting. Outside, in the wide passageway near the steps that lead up to Dr. Bowen's wartime Spherical Trig class, there are wet raincoats, umbrellas, overshoes, and Joe College, a black and brown terrier who is dry as only a dog can be who sleeps on chalky floors under vacant desks.

Inside the English classroom, nine students sit and, as students always do the first meeting of a class, appraise each

Max Steele as student—*Mills Steele*

other secretly and with an unconscious air of hostility made up of competitiveness and shyness.

No one sits in the row nearest the open windows where rain spatters on the cement window sills. No one speaks, yet there is a tension in the humid air. Mrs. Gilpatrick has not yet arrived; she has been seen at the library desk; but her reputation fills and subdues the room.

Of all the teachers on either campus, it is she who is considered the most intellectual, the most difficult in assignments, the most conservative in grading. To be sure, there are those who contend that Dr. Gilpatrick is first; it is a matter of hearsay and opinion; all that is actually known is that as a team or separately, their classroom brilliance is legend.

About Mrs. Gilpatrick, it can be said with authority that her survey courses in English literature require as much study time as any two courses put together. Her advanced grammar course is so truly difficult that it becomes an obsession with the few students who dare register for it—an aristocratic group of scholars who pore over six foot rolls of grocery paper on which they try to diagram, sometimes for five hours at a stretch, a single sentence. They each complain proudly that it is the most difficult English course ever scheduled at Furman.

In the drafty classroom, smelling now of wet clothes and wet hair, the students are silent and seem stunned. Is everyone feeling hollow in the stomach at his own audacity: the idea of writing and of reading aloud before this woman who knows every word of English literature, every nuance of English grammar, and furthermore shares with her husband a ready, though far less biting, wit? It is not too late to escape: to drop the course.

But it is; for at that moment, she enters the room talking to Eleanor Turner, the tenth, and unappraised rival. She extends her remarks, in a voice now full of laughter, to include Eleanor and the entire class: "So you see, Miss Turner, if we have all these brave souls seated here, it can't possibly be as bad as you anticipate."

Mrs. Meta Eppler Gilpatrick—*Furman University Magazine*

She is cradling to her bosom a double stack of books, fringed each along the top edge with slips of paper. She bends and lets the books as gently as a baby to the desk, steadying them there with first one, then the other, protective palm as she removes her brown hat and brown coat. Her hair and clothes are drab in a no-nonsense fashion. Yes, the British would accept her completely. "Now, let's see who we have here. Mr. Pendleton Banks, I know. Mr. Culp, Mr. Caldwell, Mr. Reeves, Mr. Steele, Miss Turner, of course. And a Miss Redwine . . ." She pauses at this delicious, un-Baptist name, hesitates, overcome by a thousand associations, smiles, then goes on. "Miss Gulesean, Miss Felkel."

The smile, the hesitation, and the promise to share her associations set the tone for the semester. The rain is steady now and enclosing. And here in this room a strange revelation is being made. Mrs. Gilpatrick, so sure of herself and her facts in other classes, is tentative and apprehensive; each word is weighed, each sentence qualified, and each definite decision (as to choice of textbook, for instance) given with apology. The authority is delicately shifted from herself as teacher to us as students. With assurance we accept the authority and condescendingly agree to subscribe to *The Atlantic Monthly*. Before the end of the hour we have sensed her respect for, and awe of, the creative process; and leave the classroom a little choked up about the literature we, at eighteen, will produce.

It rains. Each Thursday it rains. Now the windows are closed and fogged with steam; an air-hammer in the radiator beats a brassy rhythm in praise of Mr. Garrett. Overhead Dr. Bowen's class laughs. ("Take that vector and run it down to Reedy River, now run that one over to the S.A.E. House. What have you got?" He teeters on the balls of his feet, goes up on the toes, taps the board with the pointer. "What kind of angle?") There, above, all is certain. Answers are right or wrong. Here in our class all is uncertain, and ultimately, a matter of taste. We are lost.

But now we are learning to listen, not for absolutes, but for inflections. In her voice when she reads, we can hear what is so right in Eudora Welty ("An entire tree of lightning stood in the sky."), in Katherine Mansfield, and in Katharine Butler Hathaway. Now we listen for sensory detail. Through the five senses we know we are alive and through describing the world, apprehended by the five senses, we can make a fictional world live.

The rain never stops. Once for awhile in November it becomes sleet and then rain again. We are not writing stories yet, and the semester is half-over. Seasons we can describe and people, a little. And we know that the words we knew before we were five are the words that carry emotion. Who, if anyone, can deny that Mrs. Gilpatrick is no longer the teacher of stern reputation but is becoming rather a sympathetic literary mother who reads to us? She reads and with that remarkable memory, which perhaps has crippled her own creative powers, she reads entire paragraphs looking away from the book and at the ceiling, sometimes even with her eyes closed:

"Five or six times since I was born I have heard a sentence spoken that sounded as if it were made of an entirely different substance . . . We all looked the other way, we pretended we hadn't heard, and those parentless sentences were left to starve and perish, because picked up and warmed and fed, they might have had the power to change our whole lives." Her voice has dropped and as she lowers her face there is complete silence. The magazine closes on *The Little Locksmith* and her hand presses it gently to rest.

Her hands are beginning to show age. But the olive skin of her face and throat is sensual and looks as if it would smell of powder spilled in a drawer of kid gloves. Her voice is hypnotic in its range and softness. She looks up and one is shocked, as always, by the alertness and the intelligence in her bright and rather small brown eyes. As if to soften the penetrating quality of the eyes behind the rimless glasses, she

Campus scene, Furman University, Greenville, South Carolina, 1940s—
Furman University Library

smiles and begins again: "You'll find Meredith's description
of this sort of sentence, what he calls 'arterial words' under
English Literature, on the top shelf, a red book, red and
orange . . . I remember one summer my husband and I were
in Maine on a small road and coming toward us . . ." The
class is enthralled by any mention of her husband. It is rather
like being let into the homes of movie stars. Her plundering
memory is such that we will probably never get back to the
orange and red book and so we watch the approach of the
red convertible and the woman driver in the orange dress and
hat and wait for Dr. Gilpatrick's outrageous comment one
summer in Maine.

Did she or Freud perfect free association? And as in all free
association, it may be the unimportant which is important.
Above the sound of the January rain she is speaking. Katharine Butler Hathaway has died while we were reading her
in *The Atlantic* and before she could see her book in book
form. Mrs. Gilpatrick is talking, not of Hathaway, but of writers in general, and out of the flow of words comes, without
special emphasis, a part of a sentence, ". . . compassion,
without which a writer has nothing." Perhaps accidentally,

perhaps on purpose, she looks at one student in particular, or seems to. He has used writing without mercy: as a weapon to force laughter away from himself, and as a shield behind which he can hide his extreme vulnerability. "For the world cannot be comprehended by intelligence alone, or by the senses alone. But with compassion . . ." she looks away from him and out at the rain, "one can enlarge, or hope to, one's knowledge of the world within and the reader's knowledge of the world without . . ." She looks back at him. He glares at her, feeling guilty and exposed. She looks away again and does not watch to see if he will pick up the foundling sentence.

But she has lost the train of her thought and says automatically to another student: "Mr. Banks." Mr. Banks is one of those reliable young men who can begin talking sensibly at the drop of his name. He goes off on a tangent, away from the word "compassion."

There are other Thursdays and certainly there is more rain. But there can be no formal examination. What has one learned? Not, ironically enough, a great many facts from this woman who seemingly has an endless file of them. And not, in terms of a lifetime profession, a great deal about the techniques of fiction. But perhaps something far more important has been taking place in these afternoon classes. One has learned to listen, above the sound of the rain, to an inflection in a wise woman's voice which says this is simple and true and therefore poetry; or to another inflection, a flat, bored tone, which says this is exaggerated, pretentious, not seen or felt, and is therefore unworthy. And if a man is lucky, he can, years later, read his own words and hear that voice, and know nothing much about writing in general, but a great deal about a particular passage which is giving him trouble. He can, if he has time to wait and listen carefully, hear the words in her voice and know: (certainly not as absolutely as in the math class above, but well enough) it works or doesn't work: it is true or false.

Max Steele—*John Gale Sauls*

The last day it is still raining. She cradles the books to her and pauses in the door of Main Building a moment to remember where she has left "the new Gilpatrick car." Joe College stretches stiff-legged on his side, yawns, curls his legs, stares sleepily out at the rain, yawns again and shuts his eyes. Still followed by three students and still answering questions, she chooses the walk to the circle behind the library where the bronze doughboy stands on his cement pedestal.

The car door is held open for her and she settles herself behind the wheel and lays the books carefully down. A squirrel clamps himself upside down on a water oak and begins barking. His arched tail flicks in anger. Then, for a minute, he is motionless; his eyes glass over; and he shows his gums and tongue, as pink as the ceiling-wax gums and tongue of a stuffed or artificial squirrel hinged to the bark of a tree.

The class has run overtime and the campus lights are coming on along the curved walks. Already it is five-fifteen. Any more questions will have to remain unanswered. Dr. Gilpatrick is waiting at the Woman's College, and one gathers from her tactful but nervous patience, impatiently. The car door is shut firmly on a final question; and at the sound, a flock of starlings are lifted, as if by a winter wind, into a moment's arc against the rain clouds before settling into an oak near the chapel. There for awhile they will fuss, and flutter like black leaves, before giving themselves over to the night sky. The last bus from the Woman's College comes rattling and swaying up the hill.

George Garrett

My Two One-Eyed Coaches

C oaches . . . Believe it or not, it is going to have to be a couple of athletic coaches who were the ones, the teachers who, early on, influenced me and the direction of my life most of all. Helped me to find and to begin to sort out and shape and arrange such various and sundry parts of myself (the composite that we used to call *character* and probably still ought to) as have turned out to be crucial and lasting to me in my grown-up life, including that part of my life, never wholly separate and distinct from any of the rest of it and yet never, by the same token, entirely dominating all the rest of it, either, which has been devoted to the art and craft of writing. Writing mostly fiction and poetry . . .

. . . Which reminds me. I read somewhere, in some fly-by-night magazine or tabloid not so long ago, that Kim Novak, one of my old and honored favorite stars of the silver screen, was being interviewed in her well-earned retirement and was asked what she is up to these days. She was said to have answered to the effect that she was keeping busy with a little of this and a little of that and that she was also doing quite a bit of reading in her spare time nowadays. And what was she reading? "Oh," she replied, "mostly poetry and prose."

Well, mostly I have been writing poetry and prose for the past thirty years. Of course, that includes only the years of my more or less professional "career" as a writer.

Truth is, I have been writing all my life, at least for as long as I can remember, anyway, and well before I even knew how to write letters (or spell words) on a page. In our family we were all encouraged—encouraged? *we had to;* but, in fairness, it never occurred to any of us to want not to—to make up stories and poems and plays. And it became a fine and dandy way to spend an evening, in those lean and often happy depression years, unless there happened to be something good enough to cause us to give up our own devices and gather close around the tall Philco in the corner, in chairs and sitting on the floor, to look at its elegant cathedral shape and to study the mysterious lights glinting from deep within its secret places as we listened eagerly and attentively to the miracle of human voices and of sounds and music arriving in Orlando, Florida, out of thin, if usually hot and humid, air. Otherwise we very often wrote verses and stories and little plays; and then we presented them to each other before bedtime. They derived, appropriately, from every kind of source—from events in our lives, from dreams and day-dreams, from other stories, these latter sometimes from books or from each other's evening stories or, a bit later, from the movies which, on a Saturday morning, for instance, at the Rialto Theater downtown, cost a nickel for any child under twelve. And the same for some lucky children who were over twelve but didn't look it. Or were brazen enough to lie and get away with it. Or who were willing to scrunch down and try to look and act little.

—Where is all this going? You are wondering, impatiently. Where are those coaches?

Please bear with me. I have to do it, to tell it in my way or else it will not be told at all. The coaches will arrive, with their clipboards and whistles, soon enough.

Here's a coach for you, though not exactly one of the two I want to tell you about. If at age twelve, you lost the right to go to the movies for a nickel—and we did, because my father was so absolute in integrity that he would not allow any of *us*, no matter what the rest of the world might be up to, to lie or cheat about anything large or small—you gained some-thing else. You could then be a Boy Scout. Which I was. And, as a Boy Scout, one of the many things you could do was put on your uniform and go to Tinker Field and serve as an usher for the Rollins College football games. Which I did. In those days Rollins had a fine football team, too good for their league, really, and a wonderful football coach. Whose name has been lost to me forever by the years and wear and tear since then. Never mind. Nameless or not, he lives in my memory. After we had seated everyone, we could take a good seat (there were always plenty left) and watch the game ourselves. For free. I used to sit close behind the Rollins bench so I could see the players up close. And the thing that surprised me most then, and still astonishes me now, maybe more so since I have logged a lot of hours on benches both as a player and a coach, the astonishing thing was how quiet and calm and orderly the Rollins bench was. Nobody ever seemed to get upset or even very excited. The coach, in a coat and tie as I choose to remember him, sat quietly like a disinterested spectator. Never raised his voice. Sometimes he would gesture, and a player would come over and kneel or hunker down in front of him. They would talk very quietly. Deadpan. You couldn't tell whether it was a situation of praise or blame.

I decided I wanted to be a coach like that and I wrote the man a letter, asking him please to tell me all about the profession of being a football coach. Back came a long and friendly and leisurely letter, treating my request seriously. A generous and warm letter. I have carried it with me for most of the rest of my life. It sits in the upper right hand drawer of the desk in my boathouse in York Harbor, Maine, even now. I wish it were here in Charlottesville so I could quote it to you.

I wish I could remember his name here and now. He was the last football coach Rollins College ever had; for they dropped football after World War II. His name has gone into my private dark with so many others, from schools and teams, from the Army and graduate school and, yes, teaching. Even coaching. I can't for the life of me summon up the name of the head coach of football at Wesleyan University for whom I worked as an assistant line coach in the 1957 season. I can see his face clearly enough and remember him pacing up and down the sidelines, an older man, looking wise with experience and more intent than worried. Truth is, he was worried. Plenty. Sometimes in his pacing he would pause in front of me and ask in an urgent whisper: "What are they *doing* out there, Garrett? *What are they up to?*" It was a while before I allowed myself to realize that, late in his career, he had lost his learned sense of the order and coherence of the game. That it had, for him, returned to its original chaos and confusion. He knew the score, but didn't have a clue what was happening or why. At fifty-six I now understand the feeling perfectly. I also understand the need to be a little furtive about sharing it.

Anyway, at twelve, briefly, I wanted to grow up and be a coach. And thanks to the coach at Rollins College I had at least some idea of what was involved. Of course, he had ruined me for one aspect of Real Life. After that I assumed that when you wrote somebody a letter, they answered. But, when I was trying to learn to play the clarinet, I wrote Benny Goodman and he never answered. Neither did Joe Louis when I wrote him.

We will get back to coaches. But first I have to explain why it never occurred to me to need anyone else, outside of life-long friends and my kinfolk, to encourage me towards reading and writing.

Which is just as well, after all, I reckon; since, outside of family and close friends, I have never (not yet) received much encouragement from anybody about writing anything. Not so that you would notice. But, you see, I never expected to, either. I didn't look for what wasn't there. And soon enough the coaches—and not only my special and favorite and influential ones, but *all* of them, including a fair share of tyrants and incompetents—would make it brutally clear that no half-decent human being possessing a pair of functioning testicles would ever be caught, dead or alive, complaining about unpleasant, painful, and inevitably unfortunate things. I guess

I owe them one and all, from the Delaney Street Grammar School kickball instructors to the coaching staff of Princeton University in the days of Charley Caldwell, the well-executed shrug of affected toughness I can offer, the run-it-out, get-up-and-shake-it-off-and-get-your-dead-ass-moving, the no-pain-no-gain philosophy that, I have to admit, didn't help me a whole lot on the playing fields to improve the level of my performance. But which, let me tell you, has enabled me to keep on trying to solve a lot of difficult writing problems while working under often-difficult circumstances and in the face of considerable indifference. For better or worse. For richer or poorer . . .

What I was trying to say is that I came to reading and writing more or less naturally. As, for example, you might come to swimming early and easily. Which, matter of fact, I did; learning to swim at about the same time I learned to walk. And here's the irony of memory for you. I can very well remember the name of the man (he was the swimming coach at Rollins College) who took me as a toddler and threw me off the end of a dock into a deep lake where I had the existential choice of sinking or swimming. And chose to swim, thank you. His name was, I swear, Fleetwood Peoples. Could I forget a name like that? More to the point, could I invent that name? For reading we had all the riches of my father's one great extravagance—an overflowing library of some thousands of books. Books of all kinds in bookcases and piles and on tables everywhere in the house. Everybody read and read. And so did I. I remember reading Kipling and Stevenson and Dickens and Scott sooner than I was able to. And you could earn a quarter for reading any one of any number of hard books that my father thought anybody and everybody ought to read.

Here I need to pause to add a few words about my father. For there were many things, more than the love of reading and writing and the gift of the ways and means to enjoy both, which he taught me by example and which at least precluded the possibility that most teachers could ever be as influential as he was. And there were other factors which, now that I am forced to think of it, must have led me to seek out coaches as teachers. Athletic teaching was the one great thing that he could not do for me. He had been an athlete and, I am told on good authority, a very good one, playing ice hockey and rowing in school and college. (Strange now to think that, among all the sports I tried and performed, those two never interested me much and then only as a most casual spectator.) And he had led, for a time, a rugged physical life, dropping out of M.I.T. to work in Utah as a copper miner. He wanted to be a mining engineer some day, but midway his money ran out; so he went to work in the mines out west; and he hoped, to save enough money to go back to school. He had a slightly mangled left hand, missing two full fingers, and bulked, powerful shoulder muscles and a sinewy eighteen-inch collar size to show for his hard years as a miner. He had his charter membership in the United Mine Workers framed and on the wall; and in the attic there was a dusty old metal suitcase full of one kind and another of ore samples he had dug out himself. But he was crippled, which was what he called it, not being ever an advocate of euphemisms. Lame was more like it, though; for he had a bad left leg and a limp left arm. Neither of which greatly impeded his apparent vigor and energy and, indeed, were scarcely noticeable unless he tried to hurry, to run, or to leap up out of a chair. His lameness came in part from an injury and in part from a severe case of polio which had almost killed him. Now he could still swim—an awkward, but powerful sidestroke; and he learned to play a pretty good game of tennis, hobbling it is true, but over-powering many good players with a hard backhand and a truly devastating and deadly forehand. He also had a quality possessed by one of his tennis heroes, Bitsy Grant. Somehow or other, in spite of all awkwardness and all disability, he would manage to return almost anything hit at him. He was hard to ace and you couldn't often get by him. When I was a boy, he was a ranked player, fairly high on the ladder of the local tennis club. Once or twice, over those years, he and a partner were number one, tops in doubles. None of which meant anything to me at the time. I was still young enough to be horribly ashamed of all that clumsy, awkward hobbling about. Young? I still wince with embarrassment to recall it; though now I have to believe that my youthful shame could never have equaled the embarrassment of his often younger and always more graceful opponents.

By the time I was born, he was a prominent, controversial, daring and, in fact, feared lawyer, Fearless himself. Together with his partner he ran the Ku Klux Klan, then a real political power, completely out of Kissimmee, Florida. And lived to enjoy the victory. Took on the big railroads—the A.C.L., the Florida East Coast, the Seaboard, and the Southern—and beat them again and again. Tried not one, but any number of cases before the U.S. Supreme Court. Yet, at the same time and always, gave hours and hours of time, without stint, to those who were once called downtrodden. Especially to Negroes, who were more downtrodden than most anyone else. When black people came to see him at home, they came in by the front door and sat in the living room like anybody else. And nobody said a word about that or any of his other social eccentricities. Because most of them, white and black, respected him and depended on him. Those who did not respect him were afraid of him. With good reason. Once in my presence (for, by his practice, all the family was included in anything that happened at our house) a deputation of lawyers from the various railroads offered him a retainer, much more money than he earned, in effect *not* to try any more cases against them. He didn't wait or consider his reply, though he surprised all of us by being polite. He thanked them for their flattering interest. He allowed as how it was a generous and tempting proposition.

"I would be almost a rich man," he said. "But what would I do for *fun?*"

And, laughing, he more shooed them than showed them out the door.

Naturally the thing I thought I needed and wanted most of

all was someone who could teach me hopping and skipping and jumping. Someone who could teach me how to run and how to throw a ball without the least hint of awkwardness. That was, I suppose, my kind of rebellion.

Besides all that, there were writers, real professional ones, on both sides of our family. On my mother's side was my grandfather's cousin, Harry Stillwell Edwards. Whom I never met or even saw, but about whom I heard all kinds of family stories. One that stuck like a stickaburr, and I liked a lot, was how Edwards, who was then postmaster of Macon, Georgia, won a $10,000 prize for his novel *Sons and Fathers*. Now that was a plenty of money, big money, even then when I heard about it. Child or not, I knew that much. But it was, as I would later learn, a huge sum, in the last years of the nineteenth century, to fall into the hands of a Southerner of most modest means. One who my grandfather always claimed owed him some modest sum of money. Didn't choose to repay it. Chose instead, as family story had it, to rent a whole Pullman Car, fill it with family and friends, and take them all to New York City. Where the money was all spent in a week or ten days. Then back to Macon and life at the P.O.

Nobody ever had to teach me anything about the potential joys and pleasures of the writer's life.

On the other side was an aunt, Helen Garrett, who wrote truly wonderful children's books and even won some national prizes for them, too. But she always wanted to be a novelist for adults, also; and somehow she never managed that.

Then there was Oliver H. P. Garrett, my father's surviving younger brother. (Another brother had been a mountain climber and a professional guide who vanished in a blizzard.) Oliver Garrett was a much decorated soldier from the Great War, newspaper reporter for the old *New York Sun*, who had interviewed Al Capone and, yes, Adolph Hitler, too, twice. First time on the occasion of the 1923 *Putsch*, from which Oliver Garrett predicted Hitler would recover and most likely come to some kind of dangerous power. Finally in the early

1930s, with the advent of sound movies, Oliver went out, at the same time as a number of other good newspaper reporters, to Hollywood to be a screenwriter. And was, I learned much later, a very good one. Wrote dozens of good and bad and indifferent films. I have in front of me a copy of *Time* for August 4, 1930, which has a review of his movie *For the Defense* and a picture of him (p. 25) and describes him as "said to be Manhattan's best-informed reporter on police and criminal matters." Adding this little personal touch: "When Paramount began its policy of trying out newspapermen as scenario writers, he was one of the first reporters to become definitely successful in Hollywood. He is fond of driving a car fast, takes tennis lessons without noticeable improvement to his game, lives simply in a Beverly Hills bungalow with his son Peter, his wife Louise. Recently finding that he was going bald, he had all his hair cut off." He was one of the uncles, and a godfather, who sent extravagant and memorable presents at birthdays and Christmas; and once in a great while he would, suddenly and without any warning, appear for a brief visit. I recall a large man with a beret (first beret I had ever seen) and a long, shiny, yellow, open car, with shiny spoked wheels and chrome superchargers. And colorful, short-sleeved shirts. And, usually, a beautiful wife or companion—there were several, of course. I remember that he could sing and play the guitar by a campfire on the beach. And most of what I know about World War I, I learned from him, from his stories of it.

Well, then. No lack of "role models" in those days. And early on, after I had announced that I intended to grow up and be a writer, I even managed to win a crucial approval. My grandfather on my mother's side, Col. William Morrison Toomer, thoughtfully allowed that it would probably be all right for me to be a writer because: "It is as good a way to be poor as any other." He added that I should not expect him to lend me any money, not after what cousin Harry did with all that prize money without bothering to pay Papa (as we called

him) back whatever he owed him. Anyway, what could he
say to me with sincerity and conviction when one of his own
five sons, my uncles, was a professional golfer and another
was a dancer? He was a little worried about what I would find
to write about, concerned about my sheltered life and lack of
experience. I must have been at most twelve years old when
we talked. Well, when the captain and only other person on
board was knocked cold and unconscious by the boom, my
grandfather, at six years of age, had managed to sail a large
schooner with a full load of cut timber successfully into
Charleston harbor. What he didn't stop to consider was that
I already planned to use him and a lot of his experiences,
whenever possible, to make up for the absence of my own.

In one sense he was right, though. Can you see that? What
I needed to learn, what I had to be taught about before I could
be myself at all and really write about any of it, was . . . life.

In school there were teachers, some very good ones as I
remember, who were kind and were interested and who, I'm
sure, tried to help me along at one time and another. But I
was always what was politely known then as "an indifferent
student," all the way through kindergarten, grammar school,
junior high, and through most of my high school years. Those
high school years (and now we are coming close to the first
of my coaches) were spent at the Sewanee Military Academy
in Sewanee, Tennessee, that lonesome, isolated, beautiful,
and changeless mountain village. The Academy, or S.M.A. as
it was known then, is no longer with us any more. But in
those days it was part, physically as well as bureaucratically,
of the complex that formed the University of the South. Originally it had served as the preparatory school for the university, and even when I went there a very large number of the
cadets aimed and planned to go to the university.

It is possible that I might as well have gone to Charleston
and the Porter Military Academy there, which had been
founded by Toomer Porter, a kinsman of my grandfather, and
which my grandfather had attended in Reconstruction years.

George Garrett as Sewanee Military Academy cadet, 1945

But I didn't want to go there, I recall, for just that reason; and, besides there were other people from my hometown who attended Sewanee or were planning to go there. A whole group of us went together on the train. Overnight to Atlanta where we changed trains. And where we urgently tried to buy clip-on black neckties; for none of us knew how to tie a tie. Then on to Cowan, Tennessee, raw and ramshackle (then as now) at the foot of the mountain. Then by a little train slowly through the woods and up the mountain to Sewanee.

Much has been written about the place of the military school in the scheme of southern education. Calder Willingham in *End as a Man* (1947) and Pat Conroy in *The Lords of Discipline* (1980) have created successful novels out of their times at the Citadel. Our President (at this writing), was one of the stars of the movie version of *Brother Rat*, all about V.M.I. And, also at the moment of this writing, the subject has proved to be very much alive and kicking, commercially viable to boot, in a fine piece by Guy Martin, an alumnus of the Baylor School in Chattanooga, appearing in the current (June 1985) issue—"The Soul of America: Golden Collector's Issue of 1985"—of *Esquire*. A basic point he makes is true enough— that within the context of the South, military school has always been considered more conventional than elsewhere and that, therefore, the military schools have not been wholly designed for and dominated by juvenile delinquents. True, we had our share of them, brutes sent off to be as far away from home as possible, to be, if possible, tamed and reformed without the stigma of reform school. And, as if to give these predators some function and sense of purpose, there was also a modest number of others, sissies in the persistent American term (remember Harry Truman calling Adlai Stevenson a "sissy"?); these latter sent off to be hardened and toughened, turned into "men." There were some of both types at Sewanee, but the majority were made of more ordinary stuff; though normalcy was tested to the quick by a schedule which began promptly, rain or shine, at 5:00 A.M. and ended with

the bugling of Taps, and lights out at Quintard Barracks, at
10:00 P.M., and all the time between (it seemed) spent in the
daze of a dead run, running, marching, gulping meals—formations, classes, inspections, military science and tactics, all
of it controlled by constant bugle calls. At one point, really
until recently, I knew, by heart and by hard knocks, every
single American military bugle call—from First Call to Taps
and including such things as Tattoo, Call to Quarters, Guard
Mount, Mail Call, Church Call—the whole battalion of cadets
marched, armed, flags flying and the band playing "Onward
Christian Soldiers" to the chapel of the University of the
South every Sunday morning regardless of creed or country
of national origin. (There were no black students in white
schools in the South in those days.) The handful of Catholics,
Jews, and, in the British terminology, Other Denominations,
were officially Episcopalians for the duration of their time at
Sewanee. A rigorous schedule, then. And rigorous regula-
tions, too. Only seniors, and then only as a special earned
privilege, were allowed to possess radios, one per room. No
point in it, anyway. There were about thirty minutes a day
when the radio could be legally turned on. Everything you
owned, folded in a precise manner and to the precise mea-
sured inch, had to fit neatly in a tin wall locker. No pennants,
pictures, or decorations of any kind whatsoever. I remember
that each cadet was allowed to possess one snapshot. Which
was to be taped in its specific place and displayed on the wall
locker. Some cadets put up a photo of a parent or parents.
Some put up a (fully and decently clad; no bathing suits allowed by any means) picture of a girlfriend. There was quite
a flap one year, as I recall, when a cadet, who grew up and
lived on a large Central Florida cattle ranch, taped up a picture of his favorite cow. This caused a great deal of contro-
versy until it was finally decided, in favor of the cadet and
the cow, by the superintendent who was a Brigadier General
of the United States Army, in fact on active duty at the time.
As were a fairly large percentage of the faculty. For these were

the years at the beginning of World War II. Military training was very serious in any event and especially at a few places in the country like Sewanee which still, in those days, could confer direct commissions on their outstanding graduates. Others went to West Point, V.M.I., the Citadel and, I swear to you, reported back that they found these places relaxed and pleasant and easy going in comparison with S.M.A.

One way or the other, it seemed in those days before the atomic bomb, we were all going to end up in the war. Some were already back with a limp or a hobble or a piece of metal plate in the head and the first one-thousand-yard stares most of us had ever seen. The Army officers and N.C.O.s on the faculty were not, outwardly and visibly, cripples at all; but clearly they were on limited service of one kind or another, most overage and easing into retirement with a final backwater tour of duty, a year or two in an odd and remote and more or less safe place. The regular, civilian faculty, who also wore uniforms and were identified by ranks, were, of course, more obviously disabled, unfit for the war which took away most of the able-bodied men. These teachers were 4-F's, one and all, for one reason and another.

We were young and healthy, training as seriously as could be for a future of infantry combat. Wearing a variation on the traditional gray and black uniforms which, as I was to learn many years later while teaching as a visitor at V.M.I., were first introduced into this country and its military traditions by Colonel Crozet, the Napoleonic French officer who served as V.M.I.'s first superintendent. These were the uniforms of Napoleon's Young Guard, in which Crozet had served, and he brought them with him. Ever after that V.M.I., the Citadel, West Point, and the mainstream military schools wore the gray wool trousers with the black stripe down the leg and variations on the choker collar, tailcoated blouse which is called a *dyke* at V.M.I. Because it was the war, at S.M.A. we dressed down, slightly, wearing for full dress a more modern blouse and, informally, a jacket resembling British battledress or what was later called the Eisenhower jacket. No more high collars and white crossbelts. Indeed, for reasons I am not certain of except that everything was scarce in those years, we no longer wore white trousers in springtime, either. Often, for field training, we turned out in loose, baggy coveralls and old Army canvas leggings. But we still had the old high-collared gray overcoat with its red-lined cape, and there were sabers and guidons at close order drill. And drill had been simplified and streamlined for the vast citizen armies of World War II. I remember that the books and manuals we used were already out of date, no longer applicable in many large and small ways to the new ceremonies and the ways and means of dismounted drill. Sometime during those years the new field manual, 22-5, *Drill And Ceremonies* came in and became the bible for everything from full-dress parade to a single cadet, under arms, reporting to an officer indoors. (Under arms you did not remove your hat, or "cover," as it was called.) In those days, though, we still stacked arms, by the numbers, linking rifles by threes, locked and twisted together with the now-vanished stacking swivels. And, in military courtesy, it was still the correct thing to address a superior commissioned officer not by his rank, but by his duty and only in the third person. Thus: "Does the company commander wish to move the company into the shade?"

So there we were, children in costumes but, in truth, not much younger than other children in costumes who were already fighting and dying in the Pacific and, soon, in North Africa, Sicily, Italy. We got V-mail from cadets who had graduated and gone on.

And there we were in the cool fog-haunted, heavily timbered mountains of East Tennessee. We were lean and if not thriving, then enduring on skimpy institutional food, for which we had to furnish our ration cards and tickets like everybody else. There were moments in those days when most of us would have cheerfully fought to the death, or mighty close to it, for the sake of a hamburger or a piece of beefsteak. Still, the university had a first-class dairy herd (as did so many southern schools and colleges in the depression and wartime); and, in the absence of any other students except ourselves, a small V-12 Navy detachment, and a few 4-F's and discharged casualties, we had all the milk and butter and cheese we could manage. Treats—a Coca-Cola, an ice cream cone—were available at the university store, the "Soupy Store," about half a mile or so from our barracks and which we were allowed to visit, providing you were not restricted to barracks for demerits or any other disciplinary or academic reason, on Sunday afternoons, following noon dinner and prior to parade formation, roughly from 1:30 to 3:30 P.M. Most of that time would be spent in line at the counter, listening to Jo Stafford records (over and over again, "Long Ago And Far Away," tunes like that on the handsome and primitive Seberg machine, or was it an early Wurlitzer?), hoping against hope to get served in time to drink or eat whatever it was that was available and which you could afford before the sound of the bugle blowing first call for parade sent everyone at a frantic, stomach-sloshing, breathless run back to barracks, to grab our rifles, our beautiful 1903-A3 Springfield rifles, and fall in for parade . . .

Please. I am not complaining. Only describing. We were, with a precious few exceptions, too young, too ignorant and innocent, to complain about anything seriously. Growing up in the depression, coming of age in the war, we had no real luxuries to regret, nothing with which to compare, unfavorably, our busy and strictly limited little lives. Later I would find the Army mostly an easy and pleasant ride compared with those years and would begin to wonder, as I do now, how I mustered up the energy and swagger to pass through an adolescence so aggravated by rigor and deprivation.

Girls? Odd you should ask. There were a few on the mountain, as I recall, altogether untouchable and, of course, utterly desirable. Otherwise there were formal dances once or twice a year. Some nice girls from some nice schools in Chattanooga and Nashville might be brought in by bus. Spic and span, barbered, scrubbed and brushed, shined and polished, we timidly met them at the gym and tried to fill out our dance cards (yes!) before the music began to play. I remember half-lights and the scattered reflections of a rotating ceiling globe. I remember how the whole gym seemed to seethe with the exotic odors of powder and perfumes. I think the little band must have played "Body And Soul" over and over again. I remember a lot of standing and watching from the sidelines. There were some wise cadets, old timers, who, given the choice, chose not to attend the dance. Went to the library instead. Or enjoyed the odd peace and quiet of an almost empty barracks. Without temptation and maybe without regret.

Where did athletics come in? What about the coaches?

Well now . . .

Athletics were everything. A way to escape the drudgery (and sometimes, for new cadets and younger ones, the danger) of the afternoons in the barracks or study hall. To be on a team meant an excused absence from some mundane and onerous chores. Best of all, it allowed for occasional forays off the mountain. A trip to play another school. Where there might be a chance to get a candy bar and a Coke, a Grapette and a Moonpie, at a bus stop or country store. A chance to see girls, maybe even, with luck, to speak to one. A chance in the "contact" sports to move beyond simple competition and to heap some measure of your own fury and frustration upon some stranger who was, most likely, seeking to do the same therapeutic thing to you.

Who did we play against? It was, of course, the same set of schools and places in all sports. But when I try to summon it up, I think of team sports. Of football most of all. It seems to me we played all the time, almost as much as we practiced. I suspect now that some of the games didn't really count. Were merely game scrimmages. Who knows? I do know that it was a long season, beginning in late summer and ending in boredom and bone-weariness sometime after Thanksgiving. We sometimes played a couple of games in the same week. On the one hand we played against East Tennessee high schools—Tullahoma, Murfreesboro, Lynchberg, etc., together with tiny country schools whose names I've long since forgotten. On the other we played against the other military schools: Baylor and McCallie in Chattanooga, both of which were bigger and generally better than we were, but for whom we had sneering contempt because their military lifestyle was casual (in our view), easy going; Columbia Military Academy which was, we believed, *all* athletics with no academics worth mentioning to interfere with sports, and where the players were bigger and more numerous than anywhere else; Tennessee Military Institute, which appeared to be *really* a reform school of some kind, wire fence around it, catwalks and searchlights and shabby khaki uniforms. And always our Episcopal neighbor, St. Andrews, with its monks and its poor boys who grew their own food. When we played them we had to play barefooted because they had no football shoes. They had a considerable advantage, tougher feet from playing barefoot all the time.

Equipment . . . there the war made itself known and felt. For sports like football, which called for lots of equipment, there was only old and worn and battle-weary stuff. Those were still the days of the high-topped, long-cleated football shoes which seemed to weigh about ten pounds apiece and made everyone except the most graceful and adroit seem to waddle about like ducks on dry land. Leather helmets without face masks. (Actually the face mask was almost a decade away.) For people whose noses had been broken or whose teeth had been knocked out there were metallic half-masks called "bird cages," which no one would wear, no matter how urgently they needed to; because there were improbable horror stories of what would happen to you in a pile up if somebody on the other team grabbed your mask. There were thigh pads and hip pads and rib pads and shoulder pads, all of these hard leather and as heavy as can be. Often they seemed more trouble and danger than the injuries they were said to protect against. Football pants were heavy and bulky and baggy, except below the knee, where they ended, and made of something like canvas. Some high schools had enviable satin-like pants, but they tore easily and were deemed tacky. Our purple and white jersies were of heavy wool—oh, long before the reasonable concept of the tearaway jersey. Sweat-soaked or rained on, they became a heavy burden to carry.

The truth is, we considered ourselves lucky, though; for we had the uniforms and equipment of the university to draw on to supplement our own. Theirs, like ours, were probably at least a decade old; but it was possible to tape and patch together something for each player. Most of the time. Shoes were such a problem—remember, too, that shoes were rationed in the war; and that included football shoes—that we might have been better off following the example of St. Andrews. Instead we did the best we could with what was at hand. I was not lonely or unusual in wearing three pairs of socks and stuffing the toes of my huge shoes with old newspapers.

If this was Real Life, if this was all the world that mattered and we were in it, then coaches were urgently important to us all. Trouble was that most of them didn't *teach* anything. They exhorted and denounced, praised and blamed, honored and ridiculed, but they seldom had any practical advice or real instruction for us. Those who (somehow) already knew what to do were all right. And there were always a few athletes with great natural ability at this or that who figured out what to do by trial and error, intuition and inspiration. The rest of us ran about in shrill gangs, packs, and herds, desperately trying to make the elaborate diagrams of the coaches in our playbooks come to represent something real on the ground. The chaos of circles and Xs on paper bore very little resemblance to anything happening in fact and particular. Nobody on either team ever seemed to be where he was supposed to be. But only the most cynical and worldly-wise among us concluded that the fault wasn't ours.

A word about formations.

It took the war (simplicity of systems for military players who could not afford the time to practice much) and the growth of the professional football business in the post-war years, to simplify football. To reduce it, essentially, to uniform variations of the "T" formation. But in the early 1940s there was a great variety of formations still in use. I recall the Notre Dame box (with and without a shifting backfield), the short punt, doublewing and singlewing. And, of course, several kinds of "T" which was, anyway, one of the oldest and earliest of formations.

Many things followed from this plethora of offensive systems. The most obvious was that, other things being equal, one *formation* might simply overpower another, particularly if there were an added element of surprise involved. To guard against surprise, scouting of opposing teams, and any and all other forms of intelligence, became important. I remember that we often knew, well in advance, the names and sizes and individual playing habits of opposing players. Sometimes this information was less than reassuring. It was not, for example, cheering news to discover that you would most likely be playing opposite someone several inches taller, fifty pounds heavier, someone whose play was characterized as extremely aggressive. Many teams did exactly what S.M.A. did. They ran at least some plays from every one of the known offensive formations, what is now known as a "multiple offense," only more so. There were a number of coaching ideas behind this habit. One was that such flexibility allowed a team to switch from one offensive system to another, even during the course of a game, if the original offense was not moving the ball. It also allowed our team at least some familiarity with all the other formations thus lessening the potential impact of surprise.

By the same token, there were certain inevitable results of building an offense depending on a complex variety of formations. One of these was that there was less time to spend on *defensive* formations. This was before the two-platoon system and unlimited substitution made for the kind of specialization you see in contemporary football. Players had to play both ways. As if by unwritten rule and certainly by accepted practice, defense was kept simple and brutal. Most teams most of the time stayed in a 6-2-2-1 defense. Sometimes shifting into a five-man line in a clearcut passing situation. Or a seven-man line down at the goal line.

Another result was that there were so many plays to master, even against standard defenses, that nobody ever seemed to know them all. The starting lineup, the basic eleven players, had the advantage of specializing in only one position. But behind them were the rest of us, the scrubs (as we were called then), who would probably be used very sparingly in any game, anyway, because of the complex and limited substitution rules. I remember that these rules kept changing every year, but they never made substitution easy. For at least a year or two, if a player left the game, he could not return until the next quarter. So starting players usually played on with minor injuries. But often injuries were not minor. Scrubs, therefore, had to be ready to play at more than one position just in case and if they hoped to play at all. I was merely typical in being ready to play wingback, quarterback, and both guards, left and right. In actual games I, and the others, might be asked to fill in at other positions.

The result of *all this* was—at least for all the players and, I would guess with confidence, an almost equal situation among the coaches—a great deal of dust and confusion on the playing field. Missed assignments, on both sides, were almost the rule rather than exception. Luck, pure dumb luck, became a much more crucial factor in every game. So did tricks and trickery. Fake substitution plays were common. Fake punts and field goals were frequent. The old Statue of Liberty play was always worth a try. I seem to recall rehearsing an elaborate fake fumble play. All this nonsense only added to the general confusion and to the unpredictability of

Sewanee Military Academy coaches, 1945. Lt. Eugene S. Towles is fourth from left—*S.M.A. Catalogue, 1944–45*

the games. Upsets were so commonplace they could hardly be called upsets. With so many variable and changing factors, even a state of the art computer would be hard pressed to come up with any good clear patterns of probability.

. . . Well, now, you are surely thinking. All of that must have been wonderful training for a life in the American literary world: hard knocks, massive confusion, fake punts, fake passes and fake field goals, ceaseless trickery and treachery; and all of it depending on luck, on pure dumb luck . . .

And, once in a while, on coaching.

The coach who first reached me, taught me anything above and beyond the most basic fundamentals of the game, was Lieutenant Towles. I think. That is the name I remember. And the nickname, used by everyone except in front of himself— "Lou-Two." Let us call him that since that is what he was called.

Lou-Two was young and tall and lean, a splendid physical specimen. Except that he had somewhere lost an eye. Had one glass eye. And it was that, I imagine now, which kept him out of the war. I picture him now not in uniform, but in a neat sweatsuit, long-legged and moving about the playing field in a sort of a lope, which was either imitated from or maybe borrowed by his two loping boxers who always seemed to be at his heels. He was quick and just a little bit awkward, this latter I think because of being one-eyed. Some of the guys thought he was funny.

It was from Lou-Two that I began to learn some of the things which made a big difference in my life. I do not know if it was his intention to teach the things I learned. We sometimes learn what we want to quite beyond the intentions of pedogogy. (As Theodore Roethke put it—We learn by going where we have to go.) His concern at that time was teaching athletic skill. And that coincided with my interests. I had not the faintest notion that I might be learning things which would be transferable and could later be transformed into something altogether different—the art of writing. Athletic skill would grow, then fade later on with injuries, age, and change of interests. But attitudes and habits, together with something deeper than either, *rituals* really, would become so ingrained as to be part of my being.

At any rate I followed him into whatever sports he coached, season by season. He was one of several football coaches, an assistant; but he was head coach of boxing in winter and track in springtime. I had no particular natural ability at either of these sports. Swimming, which came easily, was my best sport. But I gave it up. To be coached by Lou-Two. I suppose I followed him because he had taken an interest in me and had encouraged me at a time when I was very eager, but very easily discouraged.

(Here I should digress—digression being the essence of my style—and admit that deep within me, even to this day, the same child, of course, lives and bides his time. As a middle-aged writer I am still easily discouraged and I still respond, with a kind of self-surrender, to encouragement and seeming interest. The difference is that now I know this about myself and am able to prepare to cope with it. Which, for example,

George Garrett in fighting
togs, about 1946

does not make indifference and rejection any less painful or
easy to bear. Far from it. But I now know the name of the pain
and have some rituals of damage control. I owe at least some
of that difference—maturity?—to Lou-Two.)

His interest in and encouragement of myself and others,
scrubs in life as well as athletics, now astonishes me more
than it did then. By and large coaches have their hands full
just teaching and encouraging the few pupils and protégés
who are already demonstrably talented and essential to the
success of any given team. Which is why the great art or craft
of contemporary coaching, at any level above the most elementary, is more a matter of careful and clever *recruiting* than
anything else. They assemble teams of the gifted and experienced and they teach refinements only. Of course, this is
one reason why, when you watch many college football
games today, you will see that the main and often crucial mis-

takes are made in matters of fundamentals—missed blocks and tackles.

But in a little school like S.M.A., where teams were so often overmatched, it was probably good sense to try to make something out of the scrubs. They could, after all, make a difference as, inevitably, the basic team and its best backup players were worn down by attrition during the long season.

I am still speaking of football. Which was my chief goal. Like every other red-blooded Southern boy. It never occurred to me, then, to doubt that playing football was the most important thing a young man could do with himself. Except, maybe, to go to the war. From track I learned to run and then to run faster and faster. From boxing's hard school I learned any number of things, some of them more than physical. But chiefly at that age and stage I learned to cultivate a certain kind of aggressiveness, out of self-defense if nothing else. And I experienced a sharper, keener sense of contact. It soon dawned on me that for the most part and most of the time football was neither as tiring nor as dangerous as boxing. From boxing I began to learn to take punishment better; to know that it was coming; to bear it. But at the same time I was learning, with the pleasure of instant and palpable results, to dish out punishment. Learned by doing, by giving and taking, that others, even better athletes, did not enjoy receiving punishment any more than I did. I learned then that there was at least this much equality and that if I went after my opponents, quickly, there were times when I could take command.

But from Lou-Two I was also learning other things which would prove useful. None of this learning was really verbal. It was a matter of feeling. It is only now, in the act of recalling it, that I am able to translate the experience into words and, thus, meaning. In those days I would have been severely challenged to be able to articulate even the most superficial aspects of my experience.

From him, first of all, I learned conditioning. Conditioning, then as now, only more so then, was more a mystery, more a matter of craft and secrets, than any kind of science. Faith and hope, I venture, had as much to do with being in shape as anything else. The same thing was true of the repair and healing of injuries in those days before there was anything called "sports medicine." Except for broken bones, the care of injuries was in the hands of trainers. Ours was the celebrated trainer of the University of the South who, for the duration, had no teams to care for. He was an ancient black man named Willie Six. It, too, was a mostly non-verbal experience. You went to his den at the university gym. After the basic amenities, you showed him your injury. He did things with heat and cold, with strong-scented and mysterious ointments and salves of his own making and with deft massage. It, too, was a vaguely religious experience. Sometimes, made whole as much by faith as treatment, I imagine, those who had hobbled in left cured and ready to play again.

Conditioning was mysterious like that. What you learned was that if you did certain things (and did without certain things) and performed certain rituals, your body would answer you by tiring more slowly and by recovering much more quickly from weariness, wear and tear. You learned to know and to listen to your body. Since all this was aimed toward the performance of a particular sport, its focus was less narcissistic than conditioning for its own sake or to improve appearance or health. The practical results of being in good shape, and, one hoped, better shape than others, showed up in performance. That, in itself, was a lesson of sorts which would carry over—that you could establish a relationship with the self of the body and the senses and could train it and teach it to work for you. And that you need not, indeed should not be crazy or tyrannical in this matter. If you overtrained or mistreated your body, you lost ground.

What was happening, even during this period of concentration upon the body, was a kind of self-transcendence. In which, gradually and inexorably, the body, one's own, became in part something separate and distinct, an apparatus, a sensory instrument designed to do things and to feel things and to accomplish certain chores. It need not be a thing of beauty. It need only be able to perform, to the extent of its own learned limits, specific tasks. Inevitably one was, ideally, observing the body-self in action from a different angle and vantage point. An early lesson in point of view . . .

The larger value of this learning experience, however, was more complex and is even less easy to articulate. As I see it now it was a matter of learning one kind of concentration, of a kind which would be very useful to an artist. Concentrating on preparation, one could not afford to waste either time or energy worrying about anything beyond that. You were too busy preparing to worry about the game (or match or meet) until its moment arrived. And when that happened, it was pointless to worry about anything else, past or future, except the present experience. You learned to concentrate wholly on the moment at hand and to abandon yourself completely to it.

And *that* made sense out of all the chaos and confusion. Wholly given over to the present, you likewise limited focus to a tight, small area. To your own small space. To what you had to do. You became, for yourself, like a single lamp burning in a dark house. You learned to live in that light and space with only the most minimal regard for or awareness of all the rest of it, going on all around you. You learned to play your part, early or late the same, and without regard for the score. Winning or losing didn't matter much.

The athletic advantages of this knowledge and concentration, particularly for an athlete who was making up for the absence of great natural skill, were obvious and considerable. Concentration alone gave you an edge and advantage over many of your opponents, even your betters, who could not isolate themselves to that degree. For example, in football if they were ahead (or behind) by several touchdowns, if the game itself seemed to have been settled, they tended to slack off, to ease off a little, certainly to relax their own concentration. It was then that your own unwavering concentration and your own indifference to the larger point of view paid off. At the very least you could deal out surprise and discomfort to your opponents.

But it was more than that. Do you see? The ritual of physical concentration, of acute engagement in a small space while disregarding all the clamor and demands of the larger world, was the best possible lesson in precisely the kind of selfish intensity needed to create and to finish a poem, a story, or a novel. This alone mattered while all the world going on, with and without you, did not.

What I am saying is that in learning how to teach things to my own body and how to use myself to advantage I was learning something deep beyond words about the nature of inspiration and of intuition.

I was learning about the beginning of what is called, poorly for lack of a better term, the creative process. I was learning this, first in muscle, blood, and bone, not from literature and not from teachers of literature or the arts or the natural sciences, but from coaches, in particular this one coach who paid me enough attention to influence me to teach some things to myself. I was (appropriately for a military school, I suppose) learning about art and life through the abstraction of athletics in much the same way that a soldier is, to an extent, prepared for war by endless parade ground drill. His body must learn to be a soldier before heart, mind, and spirit can.

Lou-Two, perhaps without realizing or intending it, initiated me. It would be another man, a better athlete and a better coach, who would teach me most and point me towards the art and craft I have given my grown-up life to. But I could not have gained or learned anything from the second man, the next coach and teacher, if I had not just come under the benign, if shadowy (for there is so much I cannot remember) influence of the first man.

A final track season, graduation; and I went my way, having so much by then absorbed what he had to teach that I took it all for granted without any special gratitude towards Lieutenant Towles or any special memory of him until now. I remember the two boxer dogs first. I fill in the man loping between them.

The next man had a certain fame. He was Joseph Brown, professor of art and boxing coach at Princeton University.

With Joe Brown I now encountered an artist, a sculptor, and a coach who had once been a great athlete. Never defeated as a professional fighter. And *just* missed being a world champion. Missed because he lost an eye in an accident while training for a championship fight. (Yes, oddly, he, like Lou-Two, was one-eyed.) As a coach, pure and simple, he had much to teach me. Or, better, there was so much to learn from him. For one thing, he was able to show me that there were things, particularly habits derived not from poor coaching but from experience, which it was already too late to unlearn. Things I would have to live with. There were things, beginning with my basic stance as a fighter, which were "wrong" and less than wholly efficient and effective. I fought out of a kind of sideways stance which allowed for a good sharp left jab and even a left hook and was an effective defensive stance, but limited the use of my right hand except in very close. He taught me how to analyze that stance (and other habits) and how, rather than discarding it and disregarding all the experience which had gone into forming it, to modify it slightly so as to take best advantage of its strengths and at the same time to compensate for its more obvious weaknesses. Compensation, that's what he showed me. How to compensate for what is and what isn't. Compensation for injury; compensation for inherent physical defect or bad habits.

What was happening, then, was the introduction of mind, of *thinking*, into a complex process which had been, until then, all intuition and inspiration, all ritual and mystery. He did not seek to eliminate these things, but he added another dimension to them.

The practical values were immediate. For instance, I soon

discovered that I was in far better physical condition than I had known. Learned that professional fighters planning on ten round fights did not spend any more time than I was spending in the gym or doing roadwork. Why, then, was I completely worn out, exhausted, after three rounds? Because I was . . . not using my head. Thinking, being aware of what was happening as it was happening, was in fact relaxing. With thought you could not so much coast as control your expense of energy. Which did not mean that you spent any less of yourself. It became, though, a question of how and when you spent your energy. The ideal was to expend exactly what you had, to be exactly on empty at the moment a given round (or the whole fight) ended.

This required a deeper, more objective consciousness of self. It also demanded a greater awareness of what was happening outside and around yourself. Football, at least serious football, was limited after my freshman year because of a serious knee injury. But, even so, I began, thanks to Joe Brown and the introduction of thinking into performance, to be aware of the wholeness of the game, of other things going on even as I was doing what I was supposed to do. With mind came choice. Vision was joined and fulfilled by revision.

From Joe Brown, both by teaching and example (he was still, close up, the best fighter I had ever seen), I began to learn the habits of professionalism, the kind of professionalism which would be demanded of me as an artist. Never mind "good" artist or "bad" artist. I even learned, through the habits of this kind of professionalism and the experience of trying and testing myself and my habits against others who also knew what they were doing, that nobody else, except maybe a critic-coach like Joe Brown who knew what was happening at all levels of his being, could honestly judge and evaluate your performance. I learned to recognize that the audience, even the more or less knowledgeable audience, never really knew what was going on. Nor should they be expected to. One soon had to pass beyond the stage of contempt for the ignorant audience and to recognize that their illusions did not make them contemptible.

I learned that in the end you alone can know and judge your own performance, that finally even the one wonderful coach-critic is expendable. He can solve a practical problem for you, problems of craft; but he cannot and should not meddle with the mystery of it.

I learned something, then, about the brotherhood of fighters. People went into this brutal and often self-destructive activity for a rich variety of motivations, most of them bitterly antisocial and verging on the psychotic. Most of the fighters I knew of were wounded people who felt a deep, powerful urge to wound others at real risk to themselves. In the beginning . . . What happened was that in almost every case, there was so much self-discipline required and craft involved, so much else besides one's original motivations to concentrate on, that these motivations became at least cloudy and vague and were often forgotten, lost completely. Many good and experienced fighters (as has often been noticed) become gentle and kind people. Maybe not "good" people. But they have the habit of leaving all their fight in the ring. And even there, in the ring, it is dangerous to invoke too much anger. It can be a stimulant, but is very expensive of energy. It is impractical to get mad most of the time.

In a sense this was not good training for the literary world. For the good camaraderie of good athletes is not an adequate preparation for the small-minded, mean-spirited, selfish, and ruthless competitiveness of most of the writers and literary types (not all, thank God) I have encountered. They do things which any self-respecting jock would be ashamed of. They treat each other as no fighter would ever dare to.

And all the time they talk about . . . *Art*. With a capital A. With a kind of public and mindless piety and genuflection.

Ever since my youth, since the days of first the shadowy Lt. Towles and then the unforgettable Joe Brown, I have been suspicious of pious amateurs.

Let me put it another way. In anecdote. All through my youth I admired many fighters. Especially Joe Louis. One of the many things I found admirable was that most of his moves (most of his craft) were so subtle as to be lost on all but the most knowledgeable fans. Once, in those days, I rode the Silver Meteor from New York to Florida, together with a young heavyweight who had just that week fought a ten-round exhibition bout against Joe Louis. I remember (still a fan and an amateur at heart) being amazed that this young fighter was not overawed. He had great respect, of course, and some awe. But even though he had been "carried," he had stood in there and traded licks with the great man.

"You know what really surprised me?" The fighter said. "His left jab. He has a very strong, fast left jab. It's his best punch, really."

Since then I have studied the films and I think that is true. Louis's jab was so good that it caused pinwheels and cobwebs in his opponents' heads long before he got around to the right hand punches that put them away.

(Try to imagine that kind of professionalism in literature.

Something like: "That Hemingway, he can do a fish story about as well as anybody around.")

From Joe Brown I also learned something of the permissible vanity of the professional. Joe had long since outgrown any of the false and foolish pride of the athlete. But he knew himself well enough to know that some of the pride was earned and all right. Once in a great while he would go to the fights in New York at Madison Square Garden or St. Nick's. If he went, he would be recognized, starting in the lobby with the old guys walking on their heels who sold programs. And the ushers. Before the main fight he would be introduced from the ring. He liked that moment even when it embarrassed him. It was a homecoming. He wrote a fine short story about it called, as I remember, "And You Hear Your Name." It was a good and true story about pride and mixed feelings.

Joe Brown was an artist and he was as articulate about his art as he was about his sport. He could talk about it, though

Joe Brown's bust of
Robert Frost

Bronze statue of Jesse Owens by
Coach Joe Brown

George Garrett as Princeton University freshman, 1947

always simply and plainly. For those who were tuned in to his kind of talk it was valuable. R. P. Blackmur, for example, used to discuss literary matters and matters of aesthetics with Joe. It was from Joe, Blackmur said, that he got one of his best-known titles—*Language As Gesture*. Which was a reversal of something I, myself, had heard Joe say: That in sculpture gesture was his language.

Many of his athletes also went, one night a week, to his sculpture class. It was, in those days before co-education came to Princeton, always a Life Class. The only place you could be sure to see a naked woman on the campus. A powerful inducement. We managed to learn a little about modeling clay and about the craft of hand and eye. For most of us what we learned was that we would never, ever be sculptors even if we wanted to. But, hand and eye, we learned some things that would carry over, despite a lack of natural talent.

Some of the intellectual lessons Joe Brown taught were brutally simple. In boxing, for example, he was fond of reminding his guys that to win in boxing you had to hit the other guy. To hit the other guy you had to move in close enough for him to hit you. No other way. One of the immutable lessons of boxing was that there was no free ride. No free lunch. To succeed you had to be at risk. You had to choose to be at risk. That choice was the chief act of will and courage. After that you might win or lose, on the basis of luck or skill, but the choice itself was all that mattered.

Or a matter of sculpture. Teaching something of the same sort of lesson. At one stage Joe was making a lot of interesting pieces for children's playgrounds. This in response to some Swedish things which were being put up in New Jersey and which, in Joe's view, while aesthetically interesting, had nothing special to do with *play*. He said a piece for a playground should be something you could play on and with. One of his pieces, I remember, was a kind of an abstract whale shape. High "tail" in the air and a slide from the "tail," through the inside of the "body" and out of the "mouth." It was tricky to

George Garrett—*Alice Garrett; Doubleday & Co.*

get to the top of the "tail." There was no one and easy way to climb there. Many different ways as possibilities. Some of them a *little* bit risky. You could fall down. So? You can fall out of a tree, too, or off a fence. Falling down is part of growing up. But worth the risk. Once at the top of the "tail" there was the wonderful, steep S-shaped slide waiting. Only right in the middle it leveled off. The experience of the slide was briefly interrupted.

Why?

"I want these kids to learn the truth," he said. "You can have a great slide, a great experience. But to do it all the way you've got to get up off your ass and contribute at least two steps of your own."

My first lesson in . . . *meaning in Art.*

As I am thinking about these things and writing about my thoughts, so much has changed. My father has been dead for many years. Lt. Towles has disappeared from my life. I have no idea where he may be, even if he is alive or dead. Truth is, I never saw him again or heard from or about him after graduation at S.M.A. And as I write this, I have news that Joe Brown died recently in Princeton. Thirty-five years and more have passed since he was my coach and teacher. And likewise the half-child, myself, who came to him to try to learn and to improve his boxing skills, is long gone also, even though, by being alive, I can still carry the memory of him, that child, and thus, also, of Joe Brown. I can summon up the sweat and stink of that gym. Pure joy of it when things went well. Pain when they did not.

There were other teachers at other times, earlier and later, to be sure. Some who were much help. But none who changed my life so greatly as my two one-eyed coaches. No others whose influence has lasted so long, of whom I think often and test myself, even now, against their tenets and examples.

Ironically, I tend to dismiss most comparisons of athletics to art and to "the creative process." But only because, I think, so much that is claimed for both is untrue. But I have come to believe—indeed I have to believe it insofar as I believe in the validity and efficacy of art—that what comes to us first and foremost through the body, as a sensuous affective experience, is taken and transformed by mind and self into a thing of the spirit. Which is to say that what the body learns and is taught is of great significance at least until the last light of the body fails.

Nancy Hale

Miss Dugan

When I was thirteen and in my first year at a Boston day school, Winsor, my life—such as it was—was saved by Miss Frances D. Dugan, assistant principal and one of the English faculty. She was little, pink-cheeked, and gentle, yet she plucked me like a brand from the burning.

Water makes a better image. I was drowning in seas of inferiority, shyness (that unfortunately did not look like shyness but rather antagonism), and despair. The way Miss Dugan rescued me was perfectly straightforward and concrete. I was enrolled in a class in English composition. The teacher, whom I will call Miss Floyd, had a naturally sarcastic voice which I took to be directed especially at me.

The week before, she had given out an assignment to the class, to make a paraphrase of Milton's sonnet "On His Blindness." This was to teach us what a paraphrase was. I read the poem, and a half-forgotten skill, from back in my childhood, sprang up in me. I made my paraphrase in the form of another sonnet. My father taught me the sonnet form as well as the villanelle, ballade, and the rest, in the kitchen when I was a little girl.

This week, Miss Floyd said that one of the class—and she named me by name—had ventured to attempt a poem paraphrasing the immortal Milton. She remarked, sarcastically, that this seemed rather an impertinence. She then tossed my poem into the waste-basket, whence I dared not retrieve it. I just about went under for the third time. Poetry was the only thing I *could* do.

Only a week before, Miss Lord, the principal, had called me into her office to tell me that my attitude was all wrong.

Class of 1926, Winsor School, Boston, Massachusetts. Miss Frances
D. Dugan is fourth from left, second row; Nancy Hale is fourth
from right, third row—*Notman Studio*

In effect, she said, I was saying no to all the school had to
offer.

I said nothing. It wasn't true. The school—*they*—were saying no to me! I didn't know how to play games, and Winsor
was great on games. My unhappiest hours were spent on the
hockey field, with not the faintest idea of what I was supposed to do, while Miss Chaplin shouted, "*Get* on down that
field, Hale, can't you?" My plight is such a familiar one in
letters that I won't go into the agonizing details.

Yet salvation was at hand (not nearly so familiar a condition). Miss Dugan, whom I did not know except as a figure on the platform at Assembly, found my poem, in some unimaginable way—she *couldn't* have gone through all the wastebaskets—and liked it. I assume she had a few words with Miss Floyd.

What I knew was that this sweet fond gentle teacher in blue—always in blue—sought me out, praised my Milton paraphrase (it can't have been very good) and so rearranged my schedule that instead of "Miss Floyd, Eng. Comp." I now had, twice a week, "Miss Dugan, Sp. Eng."

After that the skies cleared, the sun came out, and all the little waves danced. It was mostly poetry that we read. She introduced me to her beloved Blake, and took me through a broad range of English poetry. I wrote at least one poem a day, and from being a worm, became rather brash about my abilities.

However, what mattered was that now, all at once, I loved and respected the school. I, who had been termed an "undesirable influence," was now the editor of the school magazine. I was still no good at sports, but I did not any longer suffer about it. I knew I was making a contribution to the school—my poems won awards in national school contests. As a consequence I moved smoothly in the groove where I had been such a misfit.

That is my story—only one example of the workings of Miss Dugan's genius as a teacher. She possessed the gift of perceiving potential, of many different kinds, and bringing it out. Today she would be one of those who can spot dyslexia.

To me the most remarkable of all was her skillfulness at adapting herself to surroundings different from what she had previously known, and then controlling them. That old, famous, at the time rather snobbish school (at least among the pupils), did not faze Miss Dugan a particle. That it is not snobbish now, is I believe, largely the work of Miss Dugan.

Her father was a banker in Decatur, Indiana, and she grew up comfortably off, community-minded, and middlewestern. But no other kind of life, anywhere, troubled her. This first-class school in Boston, with its top-drawer pupils, its formidable array of affluent, blue-blooded trustees, not to say fine teachers, were duck soup to Miss Dugan. What she did was be gentle with them, as if what they needed was gentleness, and perhaps, in Boston, it was, for they loved her. The formidable Miss Lord visibly leaned on her. Miss Dugan, all by herself, made the school, perhaps even Boston, a more loving place.

She loved to teach, as a duck—presumably—loves to swim. "Miss Dugan, Sp. Eng." remained on my schedule for the remaining four years of my schooling. And for a year afterwards I, in my high heels and cloche hat, used to go back to the school—which I now recognized as the superb institution it was—twice a week, for our poetry sessions. She never gave up her fairly heavy teaching load, with all her administrative duties. After Miss Lord retired, Miss Dugan became principal, with, as assistant, Miss Knapp (a beauty with dark gold hair). After Miss Dugan herself retired, she went back to Decatur, Indiana, where I think her sisters lived. Out there she continued to teach—nephews and nieces, handicapped children, and a Great Books course.

She was always busy to the hilt of her capacity as a teacher, yet always found time for one more child who was wretchedly seeking a self. She found, moreover, time to stay in touch with me, wretched no longer; and doubtless with many others of her old rescuees.

Yet I can't help feeling she had a special place for me, after our years of adventuring among the English—and American—poets. She wrote me from Decatur, occasionally, telling me about the daily domestic round as well as about the Great Books curriculum. She came to see me in Virginia, I remember, and told me she had had a heart attack. It did not seem to concern her especially. "It didn't hurt," she said. I did hope she would not have another one. For I always hoped that somehow, somewhere, some time, I could do something for one who had done so inexpressibly much for me.

Winsor School students, about 1926

By that time she was spending her summers with Miss Knapp next door to me by the ocean, a wonderful stroke of luck for me. The house had first belonged to Miss Waterman, who had taught me Latin in school and years later, in the summer, Greek. Then it passed into the hands of the two ladies.

I used to go over there often, "just dropping in"; they nevertheless always seemed glad to see me. My relation with Miss Dugan was such that I knew anything I thought interested her, and then she was always so gentle, which soothed my often troubled mind.

By that time, of course, there were no more formidable Bostonians for her to gentle, only Miss Knapp; but she was a bit formidable in her own right. She had a trick of correcting Miss Dugan on the tiniest details—"Friday, not Thursday" or "No, Frances, you're wrong. It was Letty's sister, not Letty, who said that." She positively leapt on any error of fact, however unimportant, from her old colleague.

All of this Miss Dugan took with her usual gentleness. She would carefully correct an error. She stood up for herself when she was in fact correct, but gently, gently. She dealt with quibbling and carping as she had dealt with aggressiveness and stone-walling—with exquisite gentleness. There was only one setting—one environment—where her gentleness once failed her.

We three used to go swimming together, once or sometimes twice a day. We liked it best down at the cove where we swam off the glacial boulders into the chilly waters of Ipswich Bay. If it was too cold, as it often was, the temperature seldom rising above 65°, we swam in the stone quarry up the road— to me always a rather sinister spot as two people had drowned there.

At the cove, Miss Knapp would swim, with her slow, sure stroke, far out to where the lobster pot buoys bobbed. In the quarry, she would swim out into a second quarry that adjoined, at an angle, the one we entered.

Miss Dugan was no more athletic than I. That had provided a source of comfort to me over the years. In either place she and I used to paddle happily about near shore. Sometimes Miss Knapp would turn on her back and beckon to us. But we never went out very far. A short way beyond our footing was the most, soon followed by a retreat to the shallows.

One afternoon Miss Dugan, who was still pretty, in a flowered bathing suit—blue—and rubber cap adorned with a rubber flower, and I were messing about in the quarry. We strayed a little further out than usual. Suddenly I observed something queer. Miss Dugan was making so little effort to swim that she was, actually, sinking. Her legs were drifting downwards so that they were almost vertical. Her head, tipped back, was beginning to sink. Her chin was under water.

I realized abruptly that unless I did something, quick, Miss

Nancy Hale, with great-granddaughter

Dugan was going to drown. Miss Knapp was far away, out of sight beyond the cliffs that were the quarry's sides. I've got to save her, I thought. Of course I had no idea how to life-save.

By letting my feet down I found I could just touch bottom on tiptoe. Reaching out, I took hold of Miss Dugan's inertly drifting hand. "Hold on to me," I commanded her. I was not sure she could hear. "Just don't grab me! If you hold my hand I can pull you in."

Miss Dugan held on. For a moment it seemed infinitely perilous—I was so near the brink of the really deep water, where I would not be able to help her. Then I found surer footing, and began pulling Miss Dugan, whose body moved lightly in the water, on to the shore. She told me afterwards she had only been repeating Blake.

On the slab of rock that made a beach, Miss Dugan spat out the water she had swallowed. When she could speak, she said:

"My dear child, you saved my life!"

It was such a little thing I had done. I had barely accomplished it anyway.

"*You* saved *me*," I said. "This was no big deal."

"Oh, for pity's sake!" said my old schoolteacher, quite tartly. "That was my *life!*"

Houston A. Baker, Jr.
What Charles Knew

He was a tobacco brown, soft eyed, angular man. He had transformed himself from a poor, Bluefield, West Virginia, mountain boy into an American intellectual. He had crafted an Oxonian mask behind which one could only surmise black beginnings. I caught glimpses of that ethnic past in the twinkle—the almost break-loose and "signifying" laughter—of his eyes when he told us of his dissertation. The title of that work in progress, according to him, was: "Some Ontological and Eschatological Aspects of the Petrarchan Conceit." He never dreamed of writing such a work, but he enjoyed using philosophical words that he knew would send the curious among us scurrying to the dictionary. I believe he actually wrote on the *Canterbury Tales*. He intrigued us. Slowly puffing on the obligatory pipe, he would chide us for the routineness of our analyses of revered works in the British and American literary canons. He wore—always—a tie and tweed of Ivy provenance, and at the end of the first session of his "World Literature" course at Howard University in the fall of 1963, I had but one response—I wanted to be exactly like him.

The task was to prove myself worthy. I labored furiously at the beginning assignment—an effort devoted to Marvellian Coy mistresses and pounding parodies thereof. The result was a D and the comment: "This is a perfunctory effort. You have refused to be creative. There are worlds on worlds rolling ever. Try to make contact with them." I was more than annoyed; I was livid. Who did he think he was? I'd show him. My next essay would reveal (cleverly, of course) that I didn't

Houston A. Baker, Jr., as Howard University student, 1964—
Steve Zweig Studios

give a tinker's damn for his grade or his comments. "Creative"—Indeed!

At the conclusion of his initial class, he said: "I want you to take these texts home and have intercourse with them and derive a satisfying orgasm." The sharp and shocked intake of breath from all of us surely kept us from seeing the merriment playing over his face. I had scant wisdom vis-à-vis orgasm, and I didn't have a clue what he considered creative. So I followed the general American procedure for such cases: I winged it.

My second essay might properly have been entitled: Love's labor loosed on William Blake. I strained to see every nuance of the *Songs of Innocence*. I combed the poems for every mad hint that would help forward my own mad argument. I never turned my eyes from the text as I sought to construct the most infuriating (yet plausible) analysis imaginable. I felt my feet dancing to Muhammed Ali rhythms as I slaved away, darting logical jabs at Professor C. Watkins who would (I was certain) be utterly undone when I threw my irreverent straight right. The paper came back with the comment: "This is a maverick argument, but stubbornly logical—'A −'." Bingo! The grade in itself gave me almost enough courage to seek him out during office hours—but not quite. I corralled a friend to make the pilgrimage with me.

He was extraordinarily gracious on the mid-autumn afternoon when we had our first long talk. "Come in Mr. Baker—Miss Pierce. How are you?" His tie was loose; he was reared back in his desk chair. There was a clutter of papers and blue books, and they provided a friendly setting for a two-hour conversation. (Apparently no one else had sufficiently overcome the effects of his intimidating intellectualism to brave office hours.) He talked easily, describing his odyssey from Ohio State to a first teaching position at San Francisco State University and then to Howard. He was currently a doctoral candidate for an Ohio State Ph.D. in English. He was serving time, so to speak, at Howard until his dissertation was com-

Charles Watkins

pleted and his degree conferred. His real love was philosophy, and the New World metaphysics of Emerson set his
blood warming and brought out his best polemical instincts.
He held his Howard colleagues in low esteem because they
were wedded to an old, old literary history while he was an
enlightened devotee of the New Criticism. They were rattling
Model Ts of a socio-historical approach, while he occupied a
smoothly non-referential world of the Cleanth Brooks and
Robert Penn Warren Mercedes. We were thrilled that he considered us (potentially) enough like him to invite us to visit
him and his wife two weeks hence—for dessert.

There was far more than dessert. His wife was hospitable,
witty, attractive—and white. She was the first such person I
had met. For partners in interracial marriages were not common in my hometown of Louisville, Kentucky. The evening
surprisingly took on (in my youthful imagination) the cast
of Greenwich Village "Beats" and *verboten* revelations. The
greatest stimulation, however, came when he played the Library of Congress recording of T. S. Eliot reading "The Waste
Land." In that moment, I became, willy-nilly, a party to "modernism" in its prototypical form. I was surprised and delighted. I had heard nothing like it before. The Eliotian reading initiated my habit of "listening" for poems rather than
"looking" for them. (I spent hours thereafter in the library
listening to the sounds of English, French, and American
poets. And later in the term when we were assigned "The
Waste Land" for analysis, the echoes of that evening were
constant.) I stepped into a late fall evening with an entirely
new sense of myself and of "worlds on worlds" rolling ever.

I began self-consciously to craft a critical vocabulary. (An
instructor commented at the end of one of my assignments:
"Are 'ontological' and 'eschatological' the only words you
know?") I talked in an American literature class about the
dynamics of speech and silence—with the raven as representative of the "ontological foundations" of silence—in Poe's
famous poem. I felt I had acquitted myself with verve. The
Model T in charge said: "Mr. Baker that's a lot of gobbledy-

gook." When I told Professor Watkins of the incident, he simply said: "Mr. Baker there are people here who have not read a book or had an original idea for years." (Then, I didn't know he meant not simply Howard but the entire academic world.)

I was reassured. I began to wear ties to class and abandoned my old satchel for a green bookbag. I was happy that I could appear in such attire when he called one day for my assistance. He had suffered the indignity of *two* flat tires, and his call brought me like a shot. Ironically, though, as we kneeled in the late-November snow, I noticed how threadbare *he* was. A frayed collar belied his intellectual elegance. His down-at-the-heels shoes were closer to West Virginia than Oxford. His face was prematurely kneaded and lined. I began to glean then (but only comprehended much, much later) the enormous price he had paid (and continued to pay) for his intellectual being in the world. I felt sorry for him at that instant, but also prodigiously attracted to such ascetic brilliance.

The semester rolled to a wintry climax, and I received an A for "World Literature." By the end of the term, I had made up my mind that I not only wanted to remain an English major, but also wanted to become a Ph.D.—a university professor. The project seems abundantly feasible in today's world where graduate fellowships for Afro-Americans go begging. But in 1963, it was a rare occurrence for a black person to set his sights on a traditional Ph.D.—not a doctorate in education, or social work, or physical education—but a traditional Ph.D. in arts and sciences. The person most influential in the decisions I made over the next several years was Charles Watkins. He encouraged my ambitions, guided me to fellowships, quieted my doubts, wrote letters of recommendation, and sketched vistas of intellectual work that glowed in my imagination.

I was overjoyed to see him at the Columbus, Ohio, airport in the spring of 1966. He had returned to Ohio State, where

Houston A. Baker, Jr.

he completed his dissertation and took a position as assistant
professor in English. We had a wonderful time during my
visit. We conversed on every topic of which I was capable,
including Emersonian essays. He read my fledgling poetry,
and the twinkle in his eye told me I had many rivers to cross.
He was generously complimentary of my scholarly progress,
and I knew, on leaving, that I loved this West Virginia man
who, by dint of main force, had shaped himself into an American Scholar.

News of his death came quite unexpectedly. I received it,
quite indirectly, while attending a black writers conference.
He died of heart trouble. He and I lost touch during the years
he was in Seattle. He had taken a post at the University of
Washington. I felt that he had little sympathy for my recently

acquired interests in black literature and black studies. (A lack of sympathy that was, perhaps, justified since he had received threats and ugly harassment from black power advocates at San Francisco State who were displeased with his interracial marriage and insisted that he either join them or suffer.) He was a man of the New Criticism, and I was moving under gloriously socio-historical and polemical banners of The Black Aesthetic, where referentiality was of the utmost importance. I had joyfully allied myself with black critics who were repudiating traditional, Oxonian masks—making, so we thought, the world all "new"—redefining it in BLACK terms. I felt that I had outgrown Charles. But the wisdom of hindsight allows me to see that "growth" is merely a sign for "moving things around"—outrageous posturing designed to convince those we love that we are still worthy of consideration, to solicit from them an acknowledgment of our changing sameness. I felt profoundly lonely. I also felt guilty and helpless because Charles and I had lost touch. The only thing I could offer as a gesture of appeasement and love was the dedication of my book *Singers of Daybreak*. I sent a copy to his wife with a feeling that someone I cared for had virtually vanished, leaving no tangible trace.

In the fall of 1985, however, I received a telephone call that began: "Hello, Houston, this is Rita Watkins." Charles and Rita's son Jonathan is currently employed as a Senate aide in the District of Columbia, and his mother wondered if I would mind calling him on one of my trips to Washington. She hoped I would tell him about his father because he was only nine when Charles died. I assured her that I would be happy to call. As soon as I hung up, I began to think of what I would say to Charles' firstborn. I will tell him, I believe, that Charles was a courageous black man who carved from the granite of racism and impoverishment a role for himself as master of the best that has been thought and said in the world.

He was a teacher par excellence. He knew, better than anyone I have encountered since, how to convey the worth and excitement of a demanding intellectual enterprise to a coun-

Jonathan Watkins

try boy from Louisville, Kentucky. I am certain I will tell Jonathan that his father knew consummately well how to bless, inspire, and encourage the threadbare thinkers among us. He suggested to us a scholarly ideal that he would have been both amused and delighted to see described in the following words:

> Ful threadbare was his overeste courtepy,
> For he had feten him yit no benefice.
> Nor was so worldly for to have office.
> For him was levere have at his beddes heed
> Twenty bookes, clad in blak or reed
> Of Aristotle and his philosophye,
> Than robes riche, or filthele, or gay sautre.

I can see the twinkle in his eye as he might have said: "If you substitute 'Emerson' for 'Aristotle,' Mr. Baker, you will have a fair characterization." Like Chaucer's Clerk of Oxenforde, Charles would gladly "lerne, and gladly teche" because he knew the resonant and signal pleasure of creative intellectual thought in a land of "dust and dollars." "Emerson" is, surely, an appropriate substitution. It describes, in a word, what Charles knew so very, very well.

Sylvia Wilkinson

Three Teachers

Mama George give me a nickle today for setting a spell with her. Give me a bisquit too with salt meat and damson jam. I want her to go and pull scupanons with me cause they're way up and the tree ain't got no limbs to speak of but she said seeing as is she gets all swimmy headed when she leaves the porch that I had betta get Uncle Cravon to fetch them and then we'd set on the porch and squirt seeds tween our teeth and put hulls on our tongues and blow them out in the yard.

Mama George is on the porch rocking in her regular chair. She is waiting for her dog Jack to come home from chasing rabbits. Jack and Mama George look like they are kin, even though he is a dog and she is a person. They have jaws that hang down and croked legs and their eyes don't match. Jack gets a lot of ticks out of the woods. Mama George says the ticks hang upside down like a flying trapease and when a dog or rabbit goes by they let go and drop on them. Sometimes they miss and have to climb up the tree and start all over. Jack is fat and has a wide back and they don't usually miss him and then he can't reach them. He comes home cause he knows his friend Mama George will pull off the ones he can't reach. When I see those fat brown ticks that she thumps out in the yard I can't believe they ever were little like the ones I get on me. I'd never let one stay on me long enough to get that big. I go stomp on them and kick dirt over them so Jack won't eat them. I can't stand to do it without shoes on though. I see those brown hulls off the scupanons and can't help but think they look a lot like the ticks do.

The above passage from my seventh grade Blue Horse notebook didn't sit too well with Miss Howerton, the soon-to-be-an-old-maid-no-more daughter of a funeral director and my seventh grade teacher at Carr Junior High School in Durham. I don't know what possessed me to show her that pas-

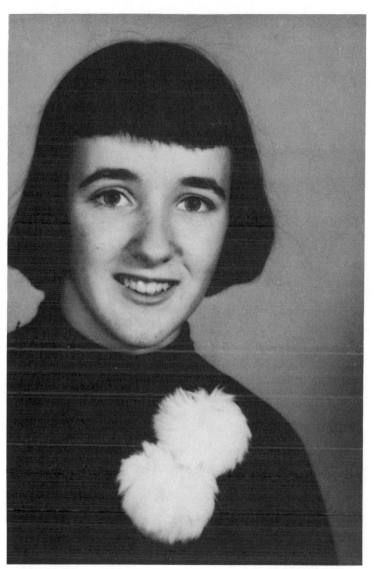

Sylvia Wilkinson as junior high student

sage. I could have shown her the one about catching bullfrog tadpoles and putting them in the drinking water, or taking home the slimy eggs with black dots and watching the tadpoles grow, or how Mama George made Uncle Cravon cut a hole through the trees so she could see the railroad tracks from her porch chair. And why her, not my parents or Sunday school, piano or dancing teacher? Or someone my age. All of those were out of the question because it had to be someone who didn't really know me.

The day I decided to come out of my writing closet and show Miss Howerton that passage was a turning point for me. It was Monday and she had been to the beach with her boyfriend. She did something very shocking for that North Carolina classroom. She turned her rear end to us and lifted up her skirt to show us her sunburned legs. They were an ugly and painful red, the kind of red you knew was going to turn to hanging, itching flesh as soon as the color faded. The boys giggled and on the playground, they said they saw her underpants which they didn't. She didn't have on stockings. It gave me a funny feeling. Grownups were supposed to tell you when to come in out of the sun, not get burnt to a crisp. We were supposed to act silly about boyfriends; teachers were supposed to be unmarried or married to deacons at the church and have no children. Also you weren't supposed to see teachers anywhere but the classroom or at church and they were never supposed to wear shorts or slacks or bathing suits, even when working in their yards, like regular people. Whatever it all meant—this brazen act—I had a brief flash that said she might like to know I was writing a book, several books at the same time, actually. I was trying to get down in writing all those stories Mama George was telling me. Mama George was counting on me because she wasn't much good at "penning" what she "meant" to say. After all, Miss Howerton had liked the poem I wrote about the black stallion where "the ship was caught in a blizzard and the captain ran around like a lizard."

I waited after school until everyone had gone. She sat painfully at her desk, though until now, I never saw the scene from her eyes. Here was this little brat, making her have to sit on those sunburned legs after her time was up while her boyfriend waited out front and she had to read something that she hadn't even asked the kid to write. I handed it to her and she read it. I still hear the gasp, see the mouth snapping shut and the face twisting as I waited for my first critic. She threw the notebook across her desk, I'm sure resisting the urge to rip it apart. It fell off the desk and I picked it up, getting swimmy-headed like Mama George.

She said: "This is disgusting." Then a pause, the eyes narrowed, and she added, "You write what I tell you to write."

If I ever had doubts about my calling—though I don't think I ever did—that sealed my fate. Like Daddy wanting me to play the piano at the church. I'd be a go-go dancer at the Proud Bird first. Or my college's motto: Educate a woman and you educate a family . . . those words have always stirred the coals of my eternal flame. "You write what I tell you to write" set me as free as splitting my cocoon, my wings drying.

Generally I had been the kid who never got singled out, at least not as "artistic" as they liked to put it in the South. I did once get picked in fourth grade for a special art class that met once a week for talented kids. I was doing a self portrait on a linoleum block when I slipped while carving my pigtails and stuck the knife through my hand; that sent the whole class back to finger painting. Sometimes I was singled out for being "unladylike"—I pushed a boy's face into a metal water fountain in third grade for picking on me and knocked out one of his front teeth. And Miss Howerton sent a note to my mother saying I had to wear dresses like a girl and it was time to hang up my corduroy pants. Yet after she read my passage, I went out and sat on the wall outside of school and decided she must not have liked it because I used the word ain't. I learned how to deal with my critics at an early age and I had known what it was like for one brief moment to be a public writer.

Carr Junior High School, Durham, North Carolina—*John Theilgard*

Then in eighth grade I had an altogether different teacher: Miss Bishop, a tiny young woman who taught biology. I learned from her that education was like a smallpox shot; everyone has to get one but it doesn't always take. I was told a smallpox shot didn't take unless you needed it and I needed Miss Bishop. Through Mama George's teachings, I was the only one exposed to her special understanding of natural processes: the meaning of fairy rings, the years the berries were heavy before a bad winter, a false spring; an education not there for the city kids I went to school with. Mama George taught me to see all the way into every corner of my vision of the natural world and not let an insect or plant or clod of dirt escape my eye. Miss Bishop was special because so much blew through my ears like wind through a vacant house, yet still I remember every phylum of the animal kingdom she

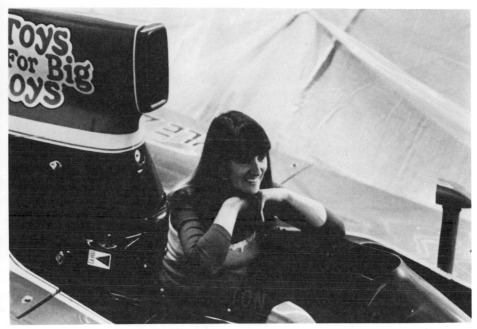

Sylvia Wilkinson in John Morton's racing car

taught me. Only fragments of Longfellow and the American Presidents are there, not a single algebra equation in the memory and regurgitation area of my mind; but after Miss Bishop and to this day I look to see if things have six or eight legs and which ones they walk or eat with.

Miss Bishop taught me to see and to draw what I saw in careful detail. She taught me words. I found out that a crawdaddy was a crayfish and a piss ant was a termite and a piss flower was a Quaker Lady and a piss dog was a poodle. Maybe the reason there were so many "piss-this-'n'-thats" was because I insisted that Mama George give everything a name. I never told Miss Bishop any of this sorting was going on, that I was putting all the natural fragments of my childhood in their proper place like pinning down butterflies by size and color and species only my butterflies were alive and wouldn't stand still for long. Miss Bishop probably wouldn't have said, "You call a jaybird what I tell you to call it," if I had told her about Mama George, but I never found out because I didn't need to. I had hours of imaginary conversations with her where she said what I wanted her to say and I impressed her with my vast knowledge of the natural world that I had gained while she lingered over her dusty books at Duke University, Ella Ruth Darwin on her voyage. I stitched up the fabric of my imagination in school and in church where I amused myself, finding the way to retreat from the order that was external by turning inside. On horseback I wove my tales coming home at night to learn the solitary business of writing in my attic room. I seriously doubt either teacher remembers me, much less knows how much she meant to me. But maybe I'm wrong, like Miss Phelps the Latin teacher: I arrived at her door on Halloween in a ghost costume, only my eyes showing and she said, "Why hello, Sylvia."

Mark Smith

A Fierce Bad Student

I had dreaded high school almost as much as I was eager to get on with the next stage of growing up. The thought of my trudging up to that yellow brick high school where it spread out like some great prison-factory along the only knoll in the surrounding flat Chicago landscape was enough to stir up primordial gnawings. These were probably no more than the usual fear of classmates older and more initiated than myself, and as yet unknown. Would the girls reject me? The varsity footballers bully me? Would I find myself sitting at an accursed table in the lunchroom, a target for flying food? I had seen enough of human nature as it had been revealed to me in my peers to know that such apprehensions of rejection and intimidation were not misplaced. High school would be a testing ground of courage and self-esteem. My intelligence and scholarship were not at stake. I gave no thought whatsoever to my future teachers. After all, what did I have to fear on their account?

I had received an excellent public grammar school education in five different schools in Michigan and Illinois. To a woman, my teachers had been no-nonsense Midwesterners for whom teaching was a commitment and a profession. They encouraged their students, invited inquiry and discussion, and saw the greatest virtue in possessing knowledge. And what yeomanlike names they had answered to: Boyd, Pettingill, Ward, Ingold, Burke, Cook, Harkness, Conlon, Burns, Bell, Mullins. They could have passed for the roster of some turn-of-the-century British cricket team. Most, in the parlance of the time, were old maids; half were autocrats; all were disciplinarians. They made us competent in reading and arithmetic, and seemed to emphasize the study of history and geography; large canvas maps were rolled up above every blackboard, and the globe was the shrinelike center of the classroom. We were made to feel like explorers. We worked hard in class, and even our free time in the library was spent peering through the stereoscope at fading photographs of Illyrian peasants and Calabrian villages.

I was always the most knowledgeable kid in my class, and most years I was also judged to be the brightest; my high grades reflected this. When I was the new kid, it took my teacher no more than the first day to spot my star. The Chicago Philharmonic gave me a medal for a beginner's viola solo, and I was made a member of our school quiz-down team on a radio show where I missed a chance of moving up to the Quiz Kids when Chicago radioland discovered I was ignorant of the fact that "What hath God wrought?" were the first words sent over the telegraph. In the eighth grade I was quarterback of the school football team and was elected president of the student council. I was also appointed class poet. Although I never thought of myself as being well rounded, I suppose I must have seemed so. On paper, anyway. In the seventh grade I had taken an examination that had placed me at the level of a college freshman in every subject but mathematics, where I held my own with a high school senior. Had I taken this same test as a high school senior, I could not have placed any higher. It is even possible that I would have regressed.

To celebrate my wintry midyear graduation from grammar school, I ate the first pizza of my life and, afterwards at home, helped myself to the bottle of incredibly sour red Bordeaux I found in the back of our refrigerator. In the dark hours of the next morning I awoke in agony: during my nightmares someone had slipped a spear into my side. A few hours later my appendix was removed. In consequence I began high school two weeks later than my fellow frosh. In a Chicago high

school with an enrollment of two thousand, I was to consti-
tute a freshman class of my own.

I recall a sense of bewilderment and confusion those first
days, as though I were a blind boy strangers laid hands on at
every opportunity and spun around. And this amid the sur-
realism of bells, lockers, lock-combinations, room numbers,
and noisy streaming crowds that, in a twinkling, vanished,
leaving closed doors and empty corridors. I was the unknown
student, behind in every class.

The first day of my drafting class my teacher gave me a
lettering assignment that the others had done two weeks earlier. My printing had always been praised and my penmanship disparaged, so right away I had an opportunity to shine.
When I handed in my paper to the teacher where he held
court at his desk, he glanced at it, smiled and wrote an F on
it, while saying from the corner of his mouth, where he always spoke, tough-guy fashion, "How does an F suit you,
my boy?" It was the first failing grade I had received in my
life, for anything. No one had bothered to show me how one
lettered in drafting. The letters had to slant just so, not stand
straight up and down as mine had. And apparently the grade
would stand. Now I noticed that beside my desk a patch of
plaster had been demolished back to the laths. On the blackboard the teacher had written a notice in chalk: "$10 reward
for the name of boy who kicks wall." In the days following,
the size of the patch would increase.

It must have been apparent to me, from the beginning, that
I had been sent to a school where the majority of the teachers
did not teach—did not teach anything—but were like politi-
cally appointed clerks, who idled away the hours at their
desks in City Hall until they had put in enough time to collect
their pensions. This meant that you either learned the subject
matter somehow on your own or copied the tests and homework assignments from another student who seemed to
know what he was doing. Like many of my fellow students,
I opted for the latter as the easier course, although in my math

classes, where I didn't understand the subject, I had no alternative. Such a system turned the students into a corps of scribes, copying furiously during lunch hours and study halls. I doubt if the homework was much examined, or graded. At best it was checked off in the grade book, and the fewer the checks the lower the grade. Tests were rarely on what we studied, and we were rarely certain, in any case, how they were counted toward our grade.

Our course grades were entered in a report book that stayed with each student for all four years, and which he handed in to his teachers on the designated marking day. In this book was kept a complete record of the student's grades. On the day of the first marking period of each term, you could catch the teacher at the desk thumbing through a grade book to see what sort of grades the student was accustomed to receiving before putting down his own grade, too often one that did not quarrel with the grades the student had received before. Since our grammar school reputations did not follow us, the first grades we received could hound us for the next four years. Because I was so far behind at the start of my freshman year, I received two Cs and two Ds the first marking period. (Actually the marking system was not A, B, C, D, F but S, E, G, F, D, the latter, the failing grade, always entered into your report book in red ink.) These were also to be my grades at the end of the semester. Cs and Ds were to dominate my grades for the four years to come. Overnight, as it were, I had gone from the top of my class to the bottom, where I would remain throughout my stay in high school. And along the way I would come perilously close to believing that I belonged there, too.

I want to be fair about this assessment. In the eighth grade I had begun to goof off; I was more interested in calling at girls' houses in the evening and in playing sports than in acquiring any more knowledge in the classroom. The previous year I had given up the viola for the ukulele. And I had no certain goal of going on to college. My high school years coincided almost exactly with the duration of the Korean War, when most of the boys could look forward not to college but to the certain fate of being drafted into the army after graduation. This awareness must have been, in some measure, responsible for the restlessness and lack of ambition found in myself and others. Nor can I claim that I was really disappointed to have discovered myself in a school where the teachers didn't do their jobs and the students cheated, lied, and, when they could get away with it, rebelled and played.

But too many of our teachers were not merely incompetent, they were foolish, which, in some cases, may have explained their incompetence. With such teachers, the classroom was either like a nursing home with the students cast in the role of unfeeling attendants, or like a prison with the teachers in the role of unfeeling guards. Over the course of a school day, a student might have to pass between these two worlds several times, and with only the three minutes between the bells to make the transition. I used to imagine a psychiatrist in some Department of Public Education office down in the Loop whose duty it was to discover all teachers who were burned out or incorrigible, or who simply failed some very basic examination in intelligence, social intercourse, or sanity, and then assign them to our school. Either that, or the teachers themselves, because of their seniority in the system—or their acknowledged disabilities—had the power to choose our school on their own. Many of them were close to retirement, and our school must have seemed a plum, the best assignment in the system. After all, it was the newest of the city high schools, having been built just before World War II, and was set in open playing fields and prairies. The building itself was clean, the rooms airy, the floors polished, and the bright prints of German Expressionist paintings hung along the walls. Located on the outskirts of the city on the northwest side, it serviced several residential neighborhoods that had the look and feel of suburbia and that were probably among the most affluent in the city at that time; best of all, they were remote from grimy factories, street traffic, and urban crime. The students were mainly of Polish, German, and Scandinavian descent. There were no blacks.

Naturally, not all of our teachers were incompetent, and in most subjects there was at least one teacher who did the job. With the exception of French, which was taught by an authoritarian woman doctor whose last name was the same as a famous death camp, the teachers of foreign languages were generally well regarded. Their students had to study, were tested fairly on their skills and knowledge, and they also learned. At least I had excellent instruction in German, and my first wife, who had gone to the same school, learned to speak Spanish well enough to get us by the first year we lived in Spain.

Nor were all incompetent teachers foolish. Miss Newhouse, a math teacher and a major in the army reserve, was an example of this kind. She was so shy and soft-spoken that I can't remember her speaking in class, although she must have done so. She certainly taught me nothing about advanced algebra. Maybe her shyness prevented her from teaching; one wonders how she performed as a major. She was a good person, with a sweet nature, and the students liked her. They didn't give her any trouble.

Miss Thomas, the civics teacher we called Ruthie behind her back, was both incompetent and foolish. Heap-shaped, her thinning hair pinned across the bald places, and wearing lacy dresses from the 1930s, she regaled us daily with her twiddle-twaddle. Her father had been some minor city politician, and she still lived with her sister in their old neighborhood, which was now integrated and run-down. Once she told us that her sister had been called a terrible name by some black girls. Neither she nor her sister knew what the word meant. "Tell us what they said," we pleaded. "No, class, don't make me repeat it." "Please!" we implored, expecting to hear that polysyllabic incestuous epithet known to be a favorite of blacks. "Oh, very well, it was *snot*," she admitted.

Another time she made the mistake of telling us how a friend of hers had attended a Hawaiian luau party and received a lei. Hands flew up in the air all over the room. The next hour was full of leis. "Did hula girls give you leis?" "Did you have to have your leis around your neck?" "If you received too many leis all at once weren't you in danger of being smothered?" "A friend of mine went to Hawaii, Miss Thomas, and he didn't get a lei." She was naive and simple; but she was also bigoted and mean. She believed that blacks belonged to a secret society whose members ventured out on Thursdays and deliberately jostled whites—gave them the elbow at the supermarket, a little shove, perhaps, at the top of the stairs. There was always a private joke in her class, one that she was never privy to. The class didn't openly abuse her, although it could have. Maybe it was too much fun playing the adult to her overgrown and ancient child.

Mr. Hardy was a more interesting eccentric. His course in world commerce was an elective, taken for an easy grade. He was silver-haired and could have passed for a downstate Republican state senator of the period. He wore the same bright blue suit each day and shuffled when he walked. He was often surprised in the men's room with a bottle held upside down to his lips. "My cough syrup," he would explain, coughing. As if we couldn't recognize a pint of whiskey. He was often badly shaved and red-faced. He had written a book published by a vanity press, entitled *Greenbacks, Gold or Silver?*, in which he argued for or against the gold standard, I forget which. At some point of the term, each of us would take a turn at flattering him and ask him if he were the author of that well-known book *Greenbacks, Gold or Silver?* He would blush with pride and admit that he was. An isolationist and admirer of Colonel McCormick, he hated Great Britain and held it responsible for America's involvement in both wars. He seriously advanced a plan whereby America would pay for transporting all of Britain's citizens to Canada, since it would prove cheaper in the long run to have them close by where we could keep our eye on them than to pay for more wars. Since his course was a favorite of older students who had full-time jobs outside of school and needed the time to sleep, while picking up a necessary credit, the class was usually quiet. But sometimes when our conversations got out of hand, he would stomp out from behind his desk and sputter, as though choking on his collar, "You dagos! Kikes! You bunch of wops!" Sometimes we would provoke him simply to hear again this predictable response. He was vulnerable and powerless before the class, but some tacit understanding had come about over the years that if you didn't bother him, he didn't bother you, and you passed the course. After all, the only course work he demanded was to copy verbatim from the text and hand the work in for a grade. Besides, only students who were not interested in learning took his courses, and they weren't usually the troublemakers.

Other teachers suffered real abuse at the hands of their students. I had an English teacher my freshman year by the name of Miss Cobley, herself new to the school. She was a great, puffy-faced woman who didn't appear to bathe and wore dresses that were little more than rags. She lived with her mother in some tenement apartment that must have been cluttered with old newsprint and garbage. When her building burned down, she had bemoaned the loss of her beautiful wardrobe, had actually wept real tears before the class. We left her alone. But in my senior year I was invited by a great mischief-maker to visit the class he had with her. When Miss Cobley attempted to take roll, half the students stood up in their seats and pelted her with Jujubees. Then they sat down. Amazingly, Miss Cobley carried on as if nothing had happened. So did the class. Later, at some signal I didn't catch, the cannonade was repeated. Toward the end of the hour, paper airplanes were set afire and sent on their brief flights across the room.

There was also Mrs. Patterson, a music teacher, who resembled most some middle-aged Blondie of the comic strip.

She seemed to have trouble seeing and speaking and understanding and walking and even standing: her feet would
move about as though the ground was giving way beneath
her, and she would often stumble, catching an instep against
an ankle. I never saw her when she wasn't smiling. We did
pretty much as we pleased in her class. For no other reason
than to demonstrate my boldness, I once told her to go to hell
to her face. To bribe us, she would sit down at the piano and
belt out "Jada-jada-jada-jada-zing-zing-zing," as though she
believed students who listened to Chuck Berry and Fats Dom-
ino wanted more than anything to sing that song. To amuse
her, we sang just as loudly while bouncing up and down as
she did on her stool behind the keys. Today I wonder if she
wasn't affected by some medication she was taking. At the
time we merely thought her dumb and dizzy.

A world history teacher we called Mr. Z. was by far the
most notorious teacher in our school. He was swarthy and
curly-headed, with a five o'clock shadow like soot, and a
prognathous jaw from which his bottom teeth protruded over
his lower lip, which gave him the appearance of a wild boar.
He appeared to speak without moving either lips or teeth,
as though those bottom teeth were a fixed cage across his
mouth. His suit fit him as it might some beast, and his pants
were so baggy that the cuffs collected at his shoes. It was a
trick of the students to sneak up behind him, pull down his
pants and leave him standing in his boxer shorts. His classroom operated like some Latin American assembly where the
deputies milled about in noisy clusters of intrigue and con-
fabulation. If anyone sat down, it was on the top of a desk.
Although no teacher could have exercised less control over
his students, he fancied himself a policeman and carried with
him at all times his black grade book in which he would pretend to write down pluses or minuses, depending on the con-
duct observed. Sometimes we would steal this book and put
down grades of our own. A favorite trick was to gather in the
rear of the classroom and make a mass infantry charge toward

his desk, which we would push against the blackboard, trapping him in the well where he was sitting while he flailed out ineffectually with his black book, his arms too short to reach us. Mr. Z. thought of himself as a famous singer, and if we promised to behave, he would reward us with a song. He would stand in front of the class and sing in his weak and awful voice "My Old Kentucky Home" to a hushed and appreciative audience that tried to keep from snickering.

I was becoming interested in acting, and would stage dramatic heart attacks in class, like some tenor dying in Italian opera. This unnerved Mr. Z. Once, after I had fallen lifeless to the floor and the students had laid me out on top of his desk, after first pushing off his papers, I decided it would create a powerful effect if I were to suddenly roll off with my eyes closed. I had not known what a long and dangerous drop it was from a desk top to a wooden floor; I broke my glasses and was lame for a week. Mr. Z. took me aside. "Smith," he said, "I don't want you to die in my class. You can have an A if you don't come anymore." But his class was daily such a theater of the absurd, with himself cast as the classic clown, that few students wanted to miss the show. I stayed and received a B.

When a smoke bomb was set off in the back of his classroom, filling the room with a thick yellow smoke, the students saw this as a wonderful excuse to seize the fire extinguishers and spray them about the walls and ceiling. Another time he was tricked by his students into leaving the school grounds on a fool's errand and abandoning, without notice, an afternoon of classes. Finally it was a speaker hung out of his classroom window during the showing of an Erpi Classroom Film that disturbed every class in session in the building that brought the disciplinarian officer to our class. He met with us, minus Mr. Z. "You are costing that man his job!" he complained. But he also made this admission: "You and I both know that man has no business teaching!"

It was hard to feel sorry for Mr. Z. He taught no subject;

we read no text, were engaged in no project; there was absolutely nothing for us to do. Occasionally he would spring
a quiz on us, always twenty-five true or false questions, five
true answers alternating with five false. We made certain to
marvel at how quickly he could grade our quizzes; why, he
hardly had to glance at them! I have my secret coding system,
he would chuckle. He boasted of a genius IQ and that he was
one of only five men in the world who understood Einstein's
theory of relativity, an odd claim for a history teacher. He was
also shamelessly fond of certain girls. When they teased him,
he blushed and purred and became excited like a male puppy
who had been stroked.

But for every foolish teacher we could push around there
was one who kept us firmly in our place. R. Baker, the oldest
of our gym teachers, wore old-fashioned eyeglasses and char-
coal-colored cardigans that made freshmen mistake him for
the janitor. He was sixty years old, no more than five-foot-
three, with weightlifter's legs, and could have thrown the
three strongest of us across the room. In health class he ad-
vised that when we were aroused, we should take a cold
shower and run around the block until the urge passed. He
was a health-faddist and a great admirer of Bernard Mac-
Fadden, sharing that great man's belief that masturbation
turned your brains to jelly. However, he could also reason out
that if alcohol killed germs on your skin, it would also kill
germs in your stomach, and he saw nothing wrong with taking a glass of wine or two for that purpose. In baseball he
made us bat like Ty Cobb, with our hands apart on the
handle. Once in health class he denounced a civics teacher
as a Communist because she subscribed to the *Nation* or the
New Republic, I forget which. He had originally denounced
her in the faculty lounge, and still hot from his outburst, had
continued the attack before his students. This was during the
McCarthy period.

He came to bear an unforgiving grudge against our class
because of an incident with a towel. Someone had thrown a

Mark Smith, with guitar, and high school friends—*Bob Miller*

soggy towel about the shower rooms until it landed in the toilet bowl where R. Baker discovered it. Enraged, he lined us up and demanded that the guilty party come forward. No one answered. Thereafter he interrogated each of us alone by turns, entreating us to confess and, when that failed, inviting us to snitch. When this got him nowhere, he took away our gym and swimming privileges for the rest of the term and made us stand against the wall in silence while he berated or ignored us as he saw fit. He turned his students into prisoners. I suspect it hurt his feelings to discover that we would stand as a body against him, shielding someone so unmanly as to fail to come forward and admit his guilt—and that, when it came to choosing sides, it was us and him. He was especially disappointed in me, and told me so. Two years later he saw me smoking on the school grounds and reported me to the football coach, who gave me a tongue-lashing in the gym office while R. Baker sat at his desk and smirked.

Give R. Baker his due; stubbornness, bad psychology, and injured feelings did reveal a human side. But the human element was hard to find in Miss Kelly, the most hated and feared teacher who ever held me captive in a classroom. She was a mousy woman, with little beady eyes that shifted as they squinted. An algebra teacher, she wore every day the same faded smock over her dress, which made her look less like a teacher in the laboratory than a woman housecleaning; on her feet were bedroom slippers. She protected herself at all times with a wicked-looking wooden pointer; in her hand, it intimidated like a bull whip. Each day in class we were chosen at random to go to the blackboard and write down the algebra problems we had been assigned for homework in our textbook; most of the students, like myself, could have been writing verse in Persian for all we understood of our equations. And God help us if she ever asked us to explain how we had arrived at such a step, since more likely than not the problem had been copied from someone else. She had a habit of referring to whoever was at the board in the third person. "Oh, class, he has that wrong!" "Oh, now look what she's doing!" There was no let-up in her searching out of our ignorance; we could be singled out, discovered, and humiliated at any moment, and we spent the hour trying to hide from that extended pointer that accompanied the command, "You—to the blackboard!" And she did not distinguish much between us, either; never knew our names. She had neither pets nor whipping boys, but surveyed all with her leveling gaze; to have likes and dislikes would presume some human judgment or feeling. I swear she would have watched the impalement of infidels with the same feeling she observed the arrival of her morning streetcar. Had some ancestor of hers not emigrated, she would have been a mean nun in Ireland who took the rod to the legs of the tinker girls.

It is difficult to name the source of her power over us, or of the terror she inspired. Perhaps it was simply that, teaching us nothing, she always knew that we knew nothing, and therefore that she always had us at a disadvantage. It was the same thing that we knew. It may be that we simply feared a public caning. She claimed that some of her former students—her boys, she called them, slyly—had become pilots during World War II and had buzzed the school to salute her, dipping their wings. She mentioned this often, and a secret smile would come over her face. I can't believe that they flew over the school to greet her. They meant to scare her, settle an old score, pay her back; maybe catch her in the open in the schoolyard where they would tear her up with their propeller blades. She was never one to have elicited responses of affection from her students.

In my junior year it looked as though I was slated to have another teacher of Miss Kelly's ilk. Rumors of Miss Strandberg preceded her debut in our classrooms. Some of our teachers taunted us by saying, "In my class you're getting away with murder, but just wait until Miss Strandberg gets here!" Miss Strandberg had transferred from one of the roughest black high schools on the south side, where she had taught English for a good many years and had earned a reputation for being merciless and tough. If she had kept tough slum kids in their seats with their mouths shut, what chance did we softies have against her? None, as it turned out. She controlled the classroom completely. For a whole term no one dared to cut her class, miss an assignment, or make a peep.

She was small, long-necked, wore her blondish hair in a knotted bun, and had on so much make-up she could have passed for a circus performer. But she dressed like a professional woman, in long wool skirts and jackets, and was always very prim and proper.

She often boasted of her black students in her former high school, of how well they had done, without having our advantages. She was likely one of those teachers of the period who had encouraged her better students to work hard so they could become a credit to their race. Once, during our class, she singled out a boy from a poor family and told us how he might not have new clothes, but he always came to school with a clean face, looking his best. The boy looked as though he wanted to crawl under his seat. No question but that she was on the side of the underprivileged. She was probably the daughter of some Minnesota or Dakota farmer who voted Farm-Labor.

Miss Strandberg was anything but foolish. And anything but incompetent. She came to teach, and—whether we liked it or not—she taught us. The backbone of her instruction was the weekly vocabulary drill. Each Monday we would come to class with the collection of obscure words we had cut from the newspapers we were made to read. A class list was then made up from these words, and, after a week of study, we were quizzed on the definitions. Today it would be a rare teacher who gave vocabulary drills at this level for any more pressing goal than to help the students achieve a high SAT verbal score. There was no such test in my day, and Miss Strandberg drilled us simply because she believed you could not read, speak, or write well without the advantage of a large vocabulary, and because she had respect—if not precisely love—for the language. I became fascinated by words and their meanings, for their own sake. And she was successful with my classmates, too. We watched our vocabulary enlarge, and went out of our way to use the new words outside the classroom. Surely back on the south side there were pockets of her former students still sprinkling their idiomatic speech with words like *ennui* and *innuendo*.

We also read and memorized poetry. It was the usual fare of our time and place: "The Man with the Hoe" and "Thanatopsis," along with Whitman, Sandberg, and Vachel Lindsay. But we were also introduced to Edwin Arlington Robinson and Emily Dickinson. Those memorized poems have stuck with me, and I suspect that if I were to encounter my old classmates where they have made their homes across this continent, we would stay up into the small hours, matching each other line for line. To this day when I encounter a Yield sign while I am driving, I sing out, unconsciously:

> I will not yield,
> To kiss the ground before young Malcolm's feet,
> And to be baited with the rabble's curse.
> Though Birnam Wood be come to Dunsinane . . .

The previous year we had had a substitute English teacher—a real Englishwoman with an Oxford accent—who had tried to interest us in poetry. She was obsessed with the verse of the young English poets who had been killed in World War I in the trenches. "All our poor dead English boys!" she would exclaim, tearful. "All the best English poets of our generation!" To a young Chicagoan, her readings seemed too affected and too alien and elitist to be sincere. But in Miss Strandberg's class I discovered—or perhaps rediscovered—that I loved language, that I liked the music of words in their combinations as much as I did their meanings.

To my surprise I became Miss Strandberg's fair-haired boy. I was called upon to give the class the answer, or to read the poem the way it should be read; my essays were read as shining examples. I'm not sure why she selected me as her star literary talent. I had received many good marks from her, to be sure, but that hadn't always helped me in other classes. Maybe she saw me as a lost soul in need of salvation, a good student gone slack who needed to be put back on the path where he rightfully belonged. Maybe I simply demonstrated a good voice for reading poetry that betrayed a sensitivity for the music and the meaning. That is not to say I couldn't disappoint her. We were forced to read *The House of Seven Gables*, which I could not abide, and I could not disguise my boredom. We were also assigned to write a short story, and mine was some trashy cinematic sketch of a man sitting in a chair while a pair of hands emerged unseen from the curtains, found his neck, and strangled him. I thought it was marvelous. Until this piece, she had commented favorably on my work. This time she said nothing, and I could see how disappointed she was. Unlike so many of her colleagues, she was absolutely honest in her grading, and, in the first marking period, I received an A. I was dumbfounded. And many honor students in the class had only Bs to show for their efforts.

One day as Miss Strandberg was returning tests, she paused beside my desk. "You know, Mark, you should become a minister," she said. "You would make a wonderful preacher. Have you ever thought about the ministry as your calling?"

I must have looked surprised, amused, embarrassed, all those responses registering simultaneously in my expression. At the same time—although I was reluctant to admit it—I was pleased and flattered. Humbled, almost. And grateful. I felt good about myself.

She was right about me; she had seen through me, had found out my secret; even as she spoke, I acknowledged that. But why on earth, out of all possible careers and callings, had she picked preacherdom as my profession? Surely the suggestion was inappropriate for a young agnostic whose favorite pastimes were playing sports, singing blues and folksongs, and drinking beer. Had she glimpsed some spiritual or moral fabric in my character that escapes me to this day? More likely her choice had to do with my reading voice and my interest in language. She wanted me to have a profession where I could use both, and since she was herself a strict church-going Lutheran, a minister was for her the ultimate of professions. A lawyer would have been too profane and close to the criminal element, and I don't know what she thought of professors. And although she taught literature, I suspect poets were too Bohemian and non-utilitarian for her tastes; and novelists—well, such a prosaic occupation that could take in the likes of Dreiser and Zola would have never entered her head. No, a preacher implied high moral char-

acter and good deeds. It was in the pulpit that I would put
my feeling for language to work, spreading the gospel, helping the infirm, saving lost souls.

Some years ago I came across a story I had written in an
early grade. It was about a cow lost in a blizzard. I was
amazed at how cleanly the little thing was written, and that
it foreshadowed a vision of one's fate that would have been
at home in books I would write in years to come. It was fright-
ening to see how much the child was father of the man. The
piece was praised by my teacher, and I was sent around to
the other classrooms where I had to read the story to the little
ones. One of the teachers whose rooms I visited told me afterwards that I would someday become a writer and that she
looked forward to reading the books that I would write. Obviously, I did not forget that moment. And even though this
teacher from long ago hit closer to the mark than had Miss
Strandberg, the moment with Miss Strandberg meant more
to me, coming as it did after three years in the wilderness.
No single moment in my high school years was to mean more
to me.

I have often wondered if those years spent in the company
of incompetent and foolish teachers served any purpose: after
all, they were experience of a special sort, and writers are
always making generous allowances for experiences. Perhaps
they were even more important than a series of solid academic spellbinders who would have made me conversant in
French, turned me into a wizard with the test tubes, and
opened my eyes to the poetry in mathematics. Nevertheless,
they did come close to taking me under, and for many of my
fellow students they must have dealt a death blow to the
spirit. How could we prize learning and inquiry if such
people served as their guardians? And we may have gone so
far as to see them as representative of the professional men
and women we would encounter in the businesses, govern-
ments, and universities to come. To have forecast a series of
such dimwitties lying in wait along the path of one's lifetime

could have persuaded the best of us to put an end to education, or even to drop out of the system altogether. Fortunately, in the first year or two after graduation, we heard stories of jocks and dunces becoming academic stand-outs in college; whereas many of the well-behaved honor students were said to have flunked out, or to have been placed on probation, usually for excessive partying. We who had slept and partied for four years were ready for business. I would graduate from a university with honors.

It was my good fortune, after my experience with Miss Strandberg, to have two excellent teachers my senior year. Mrs. Perry was a comradely sort, tolerant, good-humored, warm-hearted. She taught public speaking and drama, and again, it may be that she set her eye on me because of my speaking voice. She made her students feel relaxed and allowed them to be outspoken. She even encouraged me to squeeze in at the same desk with an ex-girlfriend, the sight of which amused her. Since there were so few boys in her classes, I was certain of having a meaty role in any play we read aloud. In the school plays, I was given the romantic leads. Through her bullying I was elected treasurer of the drama club, where my only duty was to purchase ice cream. She encouraged me to attend college where I was told by my adviser that she had written me a glowing recommendation, one of the best he had seen.

Mr. Miniker taught business. He treated us as though we were intelligent and interested, and we repaid him in kind. He lectured to us as he sat casually on his desk. What little I know today about stocks, both preferred and common, insurance policies, and labor laws comes directly from that class. His was a kind of teaching that I would later discover to my surprise would be the norm in college. However, that I would first enter college as a business major was due less to his good example than to the bad works of so many of his colleagues in the arts and sciences. He was also the only teacher I remember having whose politics were liberal.

In my first two years in college I was to encounter several teachers who showed a sensitivity to literature that I found attractive and who, by awakening similar feelings in myself, steered me toward their own profession. When I transferred to a university, my professors would take approaches to literature that were academic and sometimes pedantic, appropriate for a critic-scholar but not for a fledgling writer. They led me into false ways that I would later have to expiate on my own. But that is another story.

Miss Strandberg's favorable opinion of me was seen as an aberration by some of my other teachers. Certainly my good grade didn't carry over to the next term of English where my teacher failed me the first marking period. I had to fill out a card explaining why I had failed her class, and I wrote, "Because I didn't wear my ankle wraps." The teacher, a Miss Marvel, one of those jolly plump ladies who dress Spanish and think of themselves as wits and pranksters but have absolutely no sense of humor when they observe these same qualities in someone else, demanded that I explain myself. "You said I failed because of my absences," I said. "Well, I was absent because I broke my ankle in football practice, and the coach says I broke my ankle because I didn't wear my ankle wraps." This smark-aleckness earned me another red D the next marking period, even though I deserved better.

This same Miss Marvel once announced, when we were reading Shakespeare, that whenever you came across a rhymed couplet in the bard, you could be sure that a murder was about to happen. I slumped back in my seat, shaking my head. I didn't care what she made of the disgusted look on my face. I had read enough Shakespeare to know she didn't know what she was talking about.

I like to tell people that I graduated ninety-ninth out of a class of a hundred-and-thirteen, although I suspect it was probably out of a hundred-and-thirty-three. I played football for four years and dated cheerleaders my last two. I was voted most versatile and most musical by my classmates. Most mu-

Mark Smith—*Dean Rock*

sical because I was best known for playing the guitar that had supplanted the ukulele and singing hillbilly tunes. It was prophesied that I would wind up singing with a very pretty classmate, one Betty Lee who was originally from Mississippi, on the Grand Ole Opry; you would be able to hear us on WSM out of Nashville. A girl told me I had been the runner-up among the boys for most popular.

Strange journey to have made, I say to myself, having written this as I sit here alone in my house on the coast of Maine. A novelist and teacher of English. Who no longer strums and sings and does little else but write. Or wish that he did.

John Barth

Teacher

(For Shelly, on her birthday)

I n the featureless, low-rise, glass-and-aluminum box in
which, back in the early 1960s, I taught Humanities 1
(Truth, Goodness, and Beauty) at The Pennsylvania State
University, her hand was always up: usually first among
those of the thirty undergraduates enrolled in my section.
Many were seniors from the colleges of Education, Home
Economics, Psychology, Engineering, even Forestry and Ag-
riculture, fulfilling their "non-tech elec"; Hum 1 was not a
course particularly designed for liberal-arts majors, who
would presumably pick up enough T G & B in their regular
curriculum. But Miss Rosenberg of the bright brown eyes and
high-voltage smile and upraised hand, very much a major in
the liberal arts, was there (1) because it was her policy to
study with as many as possible of that university's huge faculty, almost regardless of their subject, who she had reason
to believe were of particular interest or effectiveness; (2) because other of her English professors had given me okay no-
tices; and (3) because the rest of my teaching load in those
days was freshman composition (a requirement she'd easily
absolved) and the writing of fiction (an art for which she felt
no vocation).

Hum 1, then:

What is Aristotle's distinction between involuntary and
non-voluntary acts, and what are the moral implications of
that distinction? Miss Rosenberg?

What does David Hume mean by the remark that the rules

Miss Shelly Rosenberg, spring of 1965

of art come not from reason but from experience? Anybody? Miss Rosenberg.

What are all those *bridges* for in *Crime and Punishment*? Let's hear from somebody besides Miss Rosenberg this time. *(No hands.)* Think of it this way: What are the three main things a novelist can do with a character on a bridge? *(No hands. Sigh.)* Miss Rosenberg?

Her responses were sound, thoughtful, based unfailingly upon thorough preparation of the assigned material, and always ready. If she was not the most brilliant student I'd ever taught—I was already by then a dozen years into the profession, with more than a thousand students behind me—she was the best. Brilliance is often erratic, capricious, cranky, sometimes indolent, sometimes troublemaking. Miss R. (the Sixties weren't yet in high gear; in central Pennsylvania, at least, most of us still lectured in jackets, white shirts, and neckties and called our students Miss and Mister, as they called us Professor) was by no means docile: If she didn't understand a passage of Lucretius or Machiavelli or Turgenev, she interrogated it and me until either she understood it or I understood that I didn't understand it either. Her combination of academic and moral seriousness, her industry, energy, and animation—solid A, back when A meant A.

The young woman was physically attractive, too: her skirt-and-sweatered body trim and fit (from basketball, softball, soccer, tennis, fencing), her brown hair neatly brushed, her aforecited eyes and smile. Ten years out of my all-male alma pater, I still found it mildly exciting—diverting, anyhow—to have girls, as we yet thought of them, in my classroom. But never mind that: As a student, for better or worse, I was never personally close to my teachers; as a teacher I've never been personally close to my students. And on the matter of *physical* intimacies between teacher and taught, I've always agreed with Bernard Shaw's Henry Higgins: "What! That thing! Sacred, I assure you. . . . Teaching would be impossible unless pupils were sacred."

Now: What is the first rung on Plato's "ladder of love"? Nobody remembers? Miss Rosenberg.

All the same, it interested me to hear, from a friend and senior colleague who knew her better, that my (and his) star student was not immune to "crushes" on her favorite teachers, who were to her as were the Beatles to many of her classmates: crushes more or less innocent, I presumed, depending upon their object. This same distinguished colleague I understood to be currently one such object. She frequented his office between classes; would bicycle across the town to drop in at his suburban house. I idly wondered . . . but did not ask him, much less her. Sacred, and none of my business.

I did however learn a few things further: That our Miss R. was from Philadelphia, strictly brought up, an overachiever (silly pejorative; let's say superachiever) who might well graduate first in her 4,000-member class. That she was by temperament and/or upbringing thirsty for attention and praise, easily bruised, traumatically strung out by the term papers and examinations on which she scored so triumphantly. That her emotional budget was high on both sides of the ledger: She expended her feelings munificently; she demanded—at least expected, anyhow hoped for—reciprocal munificence from her friends and, presumably, her crushees.

Mm hm. And the second rung, anybody? *(No hands, except of course . . .)* Miss Rosenberg.

En route to her A in Hum 1 we had a couple of office conferences, but when she completed her baccalaureate (with, in fact, the highest academic average in Penn State's hundred-year history, for which superachievement she was officially designated the university's 100,000th graduate at its centennial commencement exercises), I was still Mister Barth; she was still Miss Rosenberg. She would have prospered at the best colleges in our republic; circumstances, I was told, had till now constrained her to her state university, to its and our benefit. What circumstances? I didn't ask. Now (so my by-this-time-ex-crushee colleague reported) she had seven sev-

John Barth, teaching, spring of 1965—*Joe Graedon*

eral graduate fellowships to choose from among; he believed she was inclining to the high-powered University of Chicago.

I too, as it happened, was in the process of changing universities. I neither saw, nor heard from or about, nor to my recollection thought of excellent Miss Rosenberg for the next four years.

There is chalkdust on the sleeve of my soul. In the half-century since my kindergarten days, I have never been away from classrooms for longer than a few months. I am as at home among blackboards, half-desks, lecterns, and seminar tables as among the furniture of my writing-room; both are the furniture of my head. I believe I know my strengths and limitations as a teacher the way I know them as a writer: Doubtful of my accomplishment in both métiers, I am not doubtful at all that they *are* my métiers, for good or ill.

But, autodidact, I resist being taught by others. Years of childhood piano lessons failed to "take"; later I taught myself to play jazz drums and baroque recorder, as I taught myself tennis, skiing, sailing, novel-writing, even teaching. In literature as well as in general, my school-education was harum-scarum. For the years between kindergarten and college, I can pass some of the blame for that deficiency on to a procession of well-meaning but uninspired teachers in an economically depressed, semi-rural public school system: teachers who neither messed up my head nor much educated it. Miss Ridah Collins, however, who ran a little private kindergarten in Cambridge, Maryland, back in the 1930s, was as accomplished in her corner of the profession as were my formidable, in some instances famous, Johns Hopkins professors in theirs: the aesthetician and historian of ideas George Boas, the Spanish poet Pedro Salinas and the American poet Elliott Coleman, the romance philologist Leo Spitzer, the historians C. Vann Woodward and Sidney Painter, the literary scholars Charles Singleton, Kemp Malone, Earl Wasserman, my writing coach Louis Rubin. If most of what I know I learned from my own teaching rather than from my teachers, the fault does not lie in such stars as those, but in myself.

Having learned by undergraduate trial and error that I was going to devote my adult life to writing fiction, I entered the teaching profession through a side door: by impassioned default, out of a heartfelt lack of alternatives. I had had everything to learn; the university had taught me some of it, and I guessed that teaching might teach me more. I needed time to clear my literary throat, but I was precociously a family man, college teaching (I scarcely cared where or what; I would improvise, invent if necessary) might pay landlord and grocer, if barely, and leave my faculties less abused and exhausted than would manual labor or routine office work, of both of which I'd had a taste. Teaching assistantships in graduate school had taught me that while I was not a "natural" teacher, I was not an unnatural one, either. Some of my Johns Hopkins undergraduate students knew more about literature, even about the rules of grammar, syntax, and punctuation, than I did. I pushed to catch up; accepted gratefully a $3,000-a-year instructorship in English composition at Penn State, where I taught four sections of freshman comp. Six teaching-days a week, twenty-five students per section, one composition per student per week, all papers to be corrected and graded by a rigorous system of symbols, rules, standards. That's three thousand freshman compositions a year, at a dollar per. It drove one of my predecessors, the poet Theodore Roethke, to drink. But there were occasional half-days free, some evenings, the long academic holidays and summers. I stayed on there a dozen years, moving duly through the ranks and up the modest salary scale; got novels written and children raised; learned a great deal about English usage and abusage. And I had a number of quite good students among all those hundreds in my roll-book . . . even a few superb ones.

My academic job-changes happen to have coincided with and corresponded to major changes in recent U.S. cultural history. As America moved into the High Sixties, I moved from Penn State's bucolic sprawl—still very Nineteen-Fiftyish in '65, with its big-time football, its pom-pommed cheerleaders, its more than half a hundred social fraternities, its fewer than that number of longhaired, pot-smoking counterculturals among the 15,000-plus undergraduates, its vast experimental farms and tidy livestock barns, through which I used to stroll with my three small children when not writing sentences or professing Truth, Goodness, and Beauty—to the State University of New York's edgy-urban new operation in Buffalo. The Berkeley of the East, its disruptivist students proudly called the place. The Ellis Island of Academe, we new-immigrant faculty called it, also with some pride, so many of us were intellectual heretics, refugees from constrained professional or domestic circumstances, academic fortune-hunters in Governor Nelson Rockefeller's promising land.

Those next four years were eventful, in U.S. history and mine. Jetting once a month to guest-lecture at other universities, I literally saw the smoke rise from America's burning urban ghettos. More than once I returned from some tear-gassed campus to find my own "trashed," on strike, or cordoned off by gas-masked National Guardsmen. It was a jim-dandy place, SUNY/Buffalo, to work out the decade. My marriage came unglued; I finished *Giles Goat-Boy,* experimented with hashish and adultery, wrote *Lost in the Funhouse* and "The Literature of Exhaustion," began *Chimera.* Education, said Alfred North Whitehead, is the process of catching up to one's generation. Even for autodidacts, the tuition can be considerable.

One afternoon in the Sixties' final winter I took off from Buffalo in a snowstorm for my monthly off-campus lecture, this one at Boston College. The flight was late. My Jesuit host, who was to have taken me to a pre-lecture dinner, had his hands full just getting us across the snowed-in city to the B.C. campus, where most of my audience kindly waited. Promising dinner later, he hustled me onstage to do my number and then off to the obligatory reception (invited guests only, in this case) in a room above the auditorium. Since we were running late, we skipped the usual post-lecture question period. Even so, as happens, people came forward to say hello, get their books signed, ask things.

Such as (her head cocked slightly, bright eyes, bright smile, nifty orange wool miniskirted dress, beige boots—but my host was virtually tugging at my sleeve; we'd agreed to cut short this ritual and get upstairs to that reception as quickly as courtesy allowed): "Remember me?"

For a superachiever in the U.S.A., public-school teaching is a curious choice of professions. Salaries are low. The criteria for employment in most districts are not notably high; neither is the schoolteacher's prestige in the community, especially in urban neighborhoods and among members of the other professions. The work load, on the other hand, is heavy, in particular for conscientious English teachers who demand a fair amount of writing as well as reading from the hundred or more students they meet five days a week. In most other professions, superior ability and dedication are rewarded with the five P's: promotion, power, prestige, perks, and pay. Assistant professors become associate professors, full professors, endowed-chair professors, emeritus professors. Junior law partners become senior law partners; middle managers become executives-in-chief; doctors get rich and are held in exalted regard by our society. Even able and ambitious priests may become monsignors, bishops, cardinals. But the best schoolteacher in the land, if she has no administrative ambitions (that is, no ambition to get out of the classroom) enters the profession with the rank of teacher and retires from it decades later with the rank of teacher, not remarkably better paid and perked than when she met her maiden class. Fine orchestral players and repertory actors may be union-scaled and virtually anonymous, but at least they get, as a group, public applause. Painters, sculptors, poets may labor in poverty and obscurity, but, as Milton acknowledged, "Fame is the spur." The condition of the true artisan, perhaps, is most nearly akin to the gifted schoolteacher's: an all but anonymous calling that allows for mastery, even for a sort of genius, but rarely for fame, applause, or wealth; whose chief reward must be the mere superlative doing of the thing. The maker of stained glass or fine jewelry, however, works only with platinum, gemstones, gold, not with young minds and spirits.

Sure, I remembered her: Penn State, Hum 1, hand raised. After a moment I even recalled her name, a feat I'm poor at in company. My sleeve was being tugged: the reception. So what was she doing there? She'd seen notice of my reading in the newspaper and hauled through the snow from Brookline to catch her old teacher's act. No, I meant in Boston: Ph.D. work, I supposed, somewhere along the River Chuck, that cerebral cortex of America. Or maybe she'd finished her doctorate—I couldn't remember her specialty—and was already assistant-professoring in the neighborhood? No: It was a long story, Ms. R. allowed, and there were others standing about, and my sleeve was being tugged. Well, then: Obliging of you to trek through the drifts to say hello to your old teach. Too bad we can't chat a bit more, catch up; but there's this reception I have to go to now, upstairs. You're looking fine indeed.

She was: not a coed now, but a city-looking smart young woman. Where was it she'd been going to go after Penn State? What interesting things had her ex-crushees among my ex-colleagues told me about her? Couldn't remember: only the hand invariably raised (sometimes before I'd reached my question mark) in Truth, Goodness and Beauty, the lit-up smile, and maybe one serious office conference in her senior year. Was there a wedding ring on that hand now? Before I could think to look, I was jesuited off to an elevator already filled with the invited.

As its doors closed, she caught them, caused them to re-open, and lightly asked, "May I come along?" Surprised, delighted, I answered for my host and for her: former star student, haven't seen her in years, we did her out of her Q & A, of course she may come along.

No wedding ring. But at the reception, too, I was rightly pre-empted by the Boston Collegians whose guest I was. Ms. Rosenberg and I (but it was Shelly now, and please call me Jack) had time only to register a few former mutual acquaintances and the circumstance of my being in Buffalo these days (she'd read that) and of her having left Chicago (A long story, Jack) to teach in Boston. Aha. At Boston U? Tufts? Northeastern?

The incandescent smile. Nope: in the public schools. First at Quincy Junior High, then at Weston Junior High, currently at Wayland High. She was a public-school teacher, of English. A schoolteacher is what she'd wanted to be from the beginning.

We supposed I ought to mingle with the invited. But as she'd already taken two initiatives—the first merely cordial, the second a touch audacious—I took the next four. The kindly priest my host meant to dine me informally after this reception, at some restaurant convenient to my motel, into which I'd not yet been checked. I urged her to join us, so that we could finish our catching up off company time. She agreed, the priest likewise. As she had her car with her and the weather was deep, they conferred upon likeliest roads and restaurants (One with oysters and champagne, the guest of honor suggested) and decided upon Tollino's on Route 9, not far from the Charterhouse Motel, where I was billeted. She'd meet us there.

My duty by the invited done, she did. Tollino's came through with half-shell Blue Points and bubbly; the priest had eaten, but he encouraged us to take our time (though the hour was late now) and to help ourselves. He even shared a glass with us. We tried politely to keep the conversation three-way; it was clear to all hands, however, that our patient host was ready to end his evening. Initiative Two: The Charterhouse was just a few doors down the road; Miss Rosenberg had her car. If she was agreeable . . .

Quite. The good father was excused; he would fetch me to the airport in the morning. Another round of oysters then, another glass of champagne to toast our reacquaintance. Here's to Penn State, to old mutual friends and ex-crushees, to Truth, to Goodness, to Beauty. Here's to lively Boston, bumptious Buffalo, and—where was it? Chicago, right. A long story, you said. On with it: Long stories are my long suit.

A schoolteacher is what she'd wanted to be from the beginning. Though she'd used to weep at her difficulties with higher math and was unnerved even back then by the prospect of examinations and term-papers, she'd loved her Philadelphia public-school days. At the Pennypacker Elementary School and especially at the fast-track Philadelphia High School for Girls, where straight-800 SAT scores were not rare among her classmates, Penn State's future academic superstar had regarded herself as no more than a well-above-average performer. But she'd relished each new schoolday; had spent the long summer breaks enthusiastically camp-counseling, the next-best thing to school. Unlike me, she'd had any number of inspired, inspiring teachers well before college; her freshman year at Penn State had been unexciting by comparison with her senior year at Girls' High. Even later, when she'd sought out the local luminaries and seen to it she'd got herself a sound undergraduate education, her resolution to "teach school" had never wavered. At the urging of her professors she'd gone on to graduate study in literature and art history with the University of Chicago's Committee on the Humanities; she'd done excellent work there with Edward Wasiolek, Elder Olson, Edward Rosenheim, Joshua Taylor. She'd even charmed her way into one of Saul Bellow's courses, to check that famous fellow out. But she had no ambition for a doctorate: Her objective was *schoolteaching!* (she said it always with exclamation mark and megawatt smile), and she wanted to get to it as soon as possible. On the other hand, she'd had no truck with "education" courses: Mickey-Mouse stuff, in her opinion, except for the history and philosophy of education, which she'd found engrossing. Her baccalaureate was in English; her M.A. was to have been in the humanities. Neither had she been a teaching assistant; hers was a no-strings fellowship.

I pricked up my ears. Was to have been?

Yes: She'd left Chicago abruptly after a year and a half, for non-academic reasons, without completing the degree. This irregularity, together with the absence of education courses on her transcripts, had made it necessary for her first employer, in Quincy, to diddle benignly her credentials for certification to teach in the Commonwealth's public schools, especially as she'd come to Boston in mid-academic year. She was hired, and was being paid, as "M.A. equivalent," which she certainly was.

Abruptly, you said. For non-academic reasons.

Yup. A love-trauma, only recently recovered from. Long story, Jack.

Tollino's was closing. Initiative Three: I supposed there was a bar of some sort in or near my motel, where we could have a nightcap and go on with our stories (I too had one to tell). Should we go check me into the Charterhouse and have a look?

Sure. We made the short change of mises-en-scène down the snowplowed highway in her silver-blue Impala convertible, behind the wheel whereof my grown-up and, it would seem, now seasoned former student looked quite terrific in those beige boots and that orange miniskirted dress under that winter coat. And in the motel's all-but-empty lounge I was told at last the long story and some shorter ones, and I told mine and some shorter ones, and presently I took Initiative Four.

Plato has Socrates teach in *The Symposium* that the appre-
hension of Very Beauty, as distinct from any beautiful thing
or class of things, is arrived at by commencing with the love
of, even the lust for, some particular beautiful object or person. Thence one may proceed to loving beautiful objects and
persons in general, the shared quality that transcends their
individual differences; may learn even to admire that shared
quality without lusting after it: "Platonic love." Thereby one
may learn to love the beauty of non-material things as well:
beautiful actions, beautiful ideas (a philosopher-colleague
back at Penn State, remarking to me that he could not read
without tears the beautiful scene near the end of Turgenev's
Fathers and Children where Bazarov's old parents visit their
nihilist son's grave, added, "But I weep at the Pythagorean
Theorem, too"). Whence the initiate, the elect, the Platoni-
cally invited, may take the ultimate elevator to Beauty Bare:
the quality abstracted even from beautiful abstractions. This
is the celebrated Ladder of Love, as I understood and taught
it in Humanities 1 at Penn State, Miss Rosenberg's hand
raised at every rung. Our relationship began at the top of that
ladder, with those lofty abstractions: Truth, Goodness,
Beauty. Now my (former) student taught her (former and not
always autodidact) teacher that that process is reversible, anyhow coaxial; that ladder a two-way street; that ultimate elevator—May I come along?—a not-bad place to begin.

She was and is the natural teacher that I've never been.
Distraught by the termination of her first adult love affair
(emotionally extravagant, as such affairs should be), she'd
abruptly left Chicago and her almost completed graduate degree and found asylum in Boston with a Girls' High classmate, now a Harvard doctoral candidate. In the midst of this
turmoil—and in mid-year—she entered the profession she'd
known since first grade to be her calling, and with no prior
training or direct experience, from Day One on the chair side
of the teacher's desk she was as entirely in her element as
she'd known she would be. M.A. or no M.A., she was a mas-

ter of the art; personal crisis or no personal crisis, she impro-
vised for the Quincy Junior High fast-trackers, later for the
whiz kids at Weston and Wayland, a course in literature and
art history as high-powered and high-spirited as its teacher.
She flourished under the staggering work load of a brand-
new full-time superconscientious public-school English
teacher. She throve in the life of her new city: new friends,
apartment-mates, parties, sports, explorations, dates, liai-
sons non-dangereuses—all worked in between the long
hours of preparing lesson-plans and study questions, assem-
bling films and organizing projector-slides, critiquing papers,
grading quizzes and exams, and teaching, teaching, teaching
her enthusiastic students, who knew a winner when they
learned from one. Those first years of her professional life,
which turned out also to be the healing interim between her
two most serious engagements of the heart, were the freest
and in some respects the happiest of her story thus far.

On subsequent Boston visits (No need to fetch me to the
airport this morning, Father; I have a ride, thanks) I would
meet various of her colleagues—most of them likewise en-
ergetic, dedicated, and attractive young men and women—
and a few of her students, bound for advanced placement in
the Ivy League. I would come to see just how good good
public schooling can be, how mediocre mine was, how barely
better had been my children's. Alas, I was unable to witness
my former student's teacherly performances (my new lover's,
my fiancée's, my bride's), as she'd witnessed a semester's
worth of mine. Public schools are not open to the public; anyhow my presence would have been intrusive. By all accounts
they were superlative, virtuoso. From what I knew of her as
a student, from what I had learned of and from her since, I
could not imagine otherwise.

Yet she came truly into her professional own when, after
our marriage, we moved to Buffalo—returned to Buffalo in
my case, from a honeymoon year as visiting professor at Boston University—and, beginning to feel the burden of full-
time public-school teaching, she took with misgivings a half-

time job in a private girls' high school, the fine old Buffalo
Seminary. Its non-coed aspect gave her no trouble; much as
she'd enjoyed her male students in Boston, she'd enjoyed
even more the atmosphere of the Philadelphia High School
for Girls. But the notion of private schools—"independent
schools," they call themselves—ran counter to her liberal-
democratic principles. Buff Sem's exclusiveness was not academic, as had been that of Girls' High and the Wayland fast
track; she feared it would be social, perhaps racist: a finishing
school for the daughters of well-to-do Buffalonians who
didn't want their kids in the racially and economically integrated city system.

Her apprehensions were not foundationless. Despite generous scholarship programs and sincere attempts at "bal-
ance," good U.S. private schools are far more homoge-
neous—racially, economically, socially, academically—than
our public schools are, especially our urban public schools.
But her misgivings evaporated within a week in the sunny
company of her new charges. The girls as a group were no
brighter than those at Quincy, Weston, Wayland; *less* bright,
as a group, than her fast-trackers in those public schools or
her own high-school classmates. But they were entirely lik-
able, not at all snobbish, and wondrously educable. There are
next to no disciplinary problems in a good private girls'
school, at least not in the classroom. And with only twelve or
so students per class, and with only two classes, and without
the powerfully distracting sexual voltage of coeducation at
the high-school level—what teaching could get done!

We stayed for only one academic year. My bride was not
yet thirty. But more than a dozen years later she is still remembered with respect and affection by her Seminary headmaster and by her students from that *Wunderjahr*, older now
than she was then. She had become Mrs. Barth in two respects: It pleased her to append her husband's last name to
her own (to be called "Mrs. *John* Barth," however, rightly ran-
kles her; she is herself, not Mrs. Me), and she had become

the pedagogical phenomenon her students refer to among themselves as "Barth." One does not speak of taking "Mrs. Barth's course" in myth and fantasy, or in the short story, or in the nineteenth-century Russian novel, or in the literature of alienation; one speaks of "taking Barth." For along with large infusions of the curricular subject matter, what one gets from "taking Barth" is a massive (but always high-spirited, high-energy) education in moral-intellectual responsibility: responsibility to the text, to the author, to the language, to the muses of Truth, Goodness, and Beauty . . . and, along the way, responsibility to the school, to one's teachers and classmates, to oneself.

Very little of this came via her husband. I don't doubt that "Barth" learned a few things from her undergraduate professor about the texts in Hum 1—texts on which, however, I was no authority. No doubt too her newlywed daily life with a working novelist and writing coach sharpened her understanding of how fiction is put together, how it manages its effects. But she is a closer reader than I, both of literary texts and of student essays, and a vastly more painstaking critic of the latter, upon which she frequently spends more time than their authors. The Barth who writes this sentence involves himself not at all with the extracurricular lives and extraliterary values of the apprentice writers in his charge. My concern is with their dramaturgy, not with the drama of their personal lives, and seriously as I take my academic commitments, they unquestionably rank second to my commitments to the muse. The Barth "taken" by the girls at The Buffalo Seminary, and thereafter (since 1973, when we moved from Buffalo to Baltimore and America moved from the swinging Sixties into the sobering Seventies) at The St. Timothy's School, gives them 100 percent of her professional attention: an attention that drives her to work time-and-a-half at her "half-time" job, and that is directed at her charges' characters and values as well as at their thought processes, their written articulateness, and their literary perceptivity. I'm at my best with the best of my

students, the ones en route to joining our next literary generation, and am at my weakest with the weakest. She works
her wonders broadcast; the testimonial letters—I should get
such reviews!—pile in from her C and D students as well as
from the high achievers, and from their parents. Often those
letters come from college (wimpy, the girls complain, compared to taking Barth; we thought college would be *serious*!);
sometimes they come years later, from the strong young urban professionals many of those students have become. You
opened my eyes. You changed my life.

This my friend has done for above a dozen years now at
St. Tim's, a gently aristocratic, Episcopal-flavored boarding
school in the horse-and-mansion country north of Baltimore,
which has proved a virtually ideal place for the exercise of
her gifts. She has her complaints about it (as do I about my
dear once-deadly-serious Johns Hopkins): She worries about
grade inflation; about the risk of softening performance standards; about the unquestioning conservatism of many of
her students. She freely admires, however, the general fine-
ness of the girls themselves, who wear their privileges lightly
and who strive so, once their eyes are opened, to measure up
to her elevated standards, to deserve her praise. (I have met
numbers of the best of these girls and am every time re-
minded of Anton Chekhov's remark to his brother: "What the
aristocrats take for granted, we paid for with our youth." En-
circled by a garland of them at a party at our house, Donald
Barthelme once asked my wife, "Can't I take a few of them
home in my briefcase?")

She hopes to go on with this wonderworking . . . oh, for a
while yet. She doubts she has the metabolism for a full-length
career; sometimes wonders whether she has it for a full-
length life. As her habits of relentless self-criticism and su-
perpreparation have required a half-time situation on which
to expend more than full-time energy, so—like some poets
and fictionists—she will accomplish, perhaps must accomplish, a full professional life in fewer than the usual number

of years. We feel similarly, with the same mix of emotions, about our late-started marriage, consoling ourselves with the reflection that, as two teachers who do most of our work at home, we are together more in one year than most working couples are in two. At the front end of her forties, unlike some other high-energy schoolteachers, she has no interest in "moving up" or moving on to some other aspect of education. For her there is only the crucible of the classroom—those astonishing fifty-minute bursts for which, like a human satellite transmitter, she spends hours and hours preparing—and the long, patient, hugely therapeutic individual conferences with her girls, and the hours and hours more of annotating their essays: word by word, sentence by sentence, idea by idea, value by value, with a professional attention that puts to shame any doctor's or lawyer's I've known. How I wish my children had had such a high-school teacher. How I wish I had had!

So: for a while yet. A few years from now, if all goes well, I myself mean to retire from teaching, which I'll have been at for four decades, and—not without some trepidation—we'll see. An unfortunate side effect of the singlemindedness behind my best former student's teaching is that, like many another inspired workaholic, she's short on extraprofessional interests and satisfactions. And both of us are socially impaired persons, so enwrapped in our work and each other that our life is a kind of solipsism *à deux*. We'll see.

My university's loss will easily be made up. Talented apprentice writers doubtless learn things from a sympathetic and knowledgeable coach in a well-run writing program; I surely did. But they acquire their art mainly as writers always have done: from reading, from practice, from aesthetic argument with their impassioned peers and predecessors, from experience of the world and of themselves. Where the talent in the room is abundant, it scarcely matters who sits at the head of the seminar table, though it matters some. The Johns Hopkins Writing Seminarians will readily find another coach.

But if when I go she goes too—from schooling her girls in

St. Timothy's Barth, left, and Johns Hopkins University's Barth, right, at helm of sailboat

art and life, nudging them through the stage of romance, as Whitehead calls it, toward the stage of precision, which she can't do if we put the strictures of the academic calendar behind us—*there's* a loss can nowise be made good. Writers publish; scholars, critics publish. In a few cases, what they publish outlives them, by much or little. But a first-rate teacher's immortality is neither more nor less than the words (spoken even decades later by her former students to their own students, spouses, children, friends): "Mrs. Barth used to tell us . . ."

I like to imagine one of hers meeting one of mine, some romantically sufficient distance down the road. *He* has become (as I'd long since predicted) one of the established writers of his generation; *she* is a hotshot young whatever, who's nevertheless still much interested in literature, so exciting did her old high-school English teacher make that subject. They're in an elevator somewhere, upward bound to a reception for the invited, and they're quickly discovering, indeed busily seeking, additional common ground. Somehow the city of Baltimore gets mentioned: Hey, they both went to school there! Later, over oysters and champagne, they circle back to that subject. She'd been in high school, he in graduate school: St. Timothy's, Johns Hopkins. Hopkins, did he say, in the mid-Eighties? She supposes then (knowledgeably indeed for a young international banker) that he must have worked with her old English teacher's husband, the novelist . . .

Sure, we all had Barth.

What a smile she smiles! You think *you* had Barth, she declares (it's late; the place is closing; they bet there's a nightcappery somewhere near his motel). Never mind *that* one: Out at St. Timothy's, we had *Barth*! Talk about teachers!

Let's.

Biographical Notes

Houston A. Baker, Jr., was born in Louisville, Kentucky, in 1943. He graduated from Howard University (B.A., M.A.) and Yale University, where he received the Ph.D. degree. He has taught at Howard and the University of Virginia, and is now professor of English at the University of Pennsylvania. His books include *Long Black Song, Singers of Daybreak, A Many-Colored Court of Dreams, No Matter Where You Travel, You Still Be Black, The Journey Back,* and *Spirit Run.* He has won the Alfred Longuiel Poetry Award and has received fellowships from the Center for Advanced Study, the Guggenheim Foundation, and the National Humanities Center.

John Barth was born in Cambridge, Maryland, in 1930, and studied music at the Julliard School before graduating the Writing Seminars at the Johns Hopkins University (B.A., M.A.). He has taught at Pennsylvania State University, the State University of New York at Buffalo, and Boston University, and since 1973 at Johns Hopkins. His books include *The Floating Opera, The End of the Road, The Sot-Weed Factor, Giles Goat-Boy, Lost in the Funhouse, Chimera,* and *Letters.* He has recently completed a new novel, *The Tidewater Tales.*

Fred Chappell was born in Canton, North Carolina, in 1936. He is a graduate of Duke University, and teaches at the University of North Carolina at Greensboro. His books include *It Is Time, Lord, The Inkling, Dagon, The World Between the Eyes, The Gaudy Place, Midquest, Bloodfire,* and *I Am One of You Forever.* In 1985 he was awarded the Bollingen Prize for Poetry.

John Eisenhower was born in Denver, Colorado, in 1922, attended school at various places in the United States and the Philippines, and is a graduate of the U.S. Military Academy (B.S.) and Columbia University (M.A.). Following an Army career in which he advanced to the rank of lieutenant colonel, he took up a writing career. In 1964 he was made brigadier general in the United States Army Reserve. He has been a member of the White House Staff, U.S. ambassador to Belgium, and consultant to the President of the United States. His books include *The Bitter Woods, Strictly Personal, Letters to Mamie,* and *Allies.* He has recently completed the first volume of a two-volume history of the Mexican War. He lives in Westchester, Pennsylvania.

George Garrett was born in Orlando, Florida, in 1922. He is a graduate of Princeton University (B.A., M.A.). He has taught at Wesleyan University, Rice University, the University of Virginia, Hollins College, the University of South Carolina, the University of Michigan, and is now professor of English at the University of Virginia. His books include *The Reverend Ghost, King of the Mountain, The Sleeping Gypsy and Other Poems, The Finished Man, Which Ones Are the Enemy?, Do, Lord, Remember Me, Death of the Fox, The Magic Striptease, The Succession,* and *An Evening Performance.* He has received the Prix de Rome, the *Sewanee Review* fellowship, and a Ford Foundation Fellowship.

Elizabeth Forsythe Hailey is a native of Houston, Texas, and a graduate of Hollins College. She has worked on television scripts with her husband, the playwright Oliver Hailey. Her novels include *A Woman of Independent Means, Life Sentences,* and *Joanna's Husband and David's Wife.* She lives in Studio City, California.

Nancy Hale was born in Boston, Massachusetts, in 1908, and attended Winsor School and the Boston Museum (Art) School. She has been assistant editor of *Vogue* and *Vanity Fair* magazines and a reporter for the *New York Times.* She has lectured at the Bread Loaf Writers Conference and been a Phi Beta Kappa Visiting Scholar. Her books include *The Young Die Good, Never Any More, The Prodigal Women, The Sign of Jonah, Dear Beast, Black Summer, Secrets, A New England Childhood, The Realities of Fiction, The Life in the Studio,* and *Mrs. Cassatt.* She has received the O. Henry Award, a Benjamin Franklin Citation, the Bellaman Award, and the Sara Josephs Hale Award. She lives in Charlottesville, Virginia, with her husband, the literature scholar Fredson Bowers.

Alfred Kazin was born in Brooklyn in 1915. He graduated from the City College of New York (B.S.S.) and Columbia University (A.M.). He has been literary editor of the *New Republic,* and has taught at Black Mountain College, Harvard University, Smith College, New York University, Amherst College, C.C.N.Y., State University of New York–Stony Brook, Hunter College, the University of Notre Dame, and the Graduate School of the City University of New York. His books include *On Native Grounds, A Walker in the City, The Inmost Leaf, Contemporaries, Starting Out in the Thirties, Bright Book of Life, New York Jew,* and *An American Procession.* He has received Guggenheim, National Endowment for the Humanities, and Ford fellowships, and has been Senior Fellow at the Center for Advanced Study in the Behavioral Sciences. His awards include the George Polk Memorial and the Brandeis University Creative Arts awards as well as the Jay B. Hubbell Medal. He lives in New York City.

Louis D. Rubin, Jr., was born in Charleston, South Carolina, in 1923. He graduated from the University of Richmond (B.A.) and the Johns Hopkins University (M.A., Ph.D.). He has been executive secretary of the American Studies Association and has taught at Johns Hopkins and Hollins College, and is professor of English at the University of North Carolina at Chapel Hill. He has been awarded Guggenheim and American Council of Learned Societies fellowships, and two of his short stories have appeared in the *Best American Short Stories* collections. He is editor of the Southern Literary Studies Series of the Louisiana State University Press. He has published two novels, *The Golden Weather* and *Surfaces of a Diamond*, as well as books on Southern and American literature and history, including *Thomas Wolfe: The Weather of His Youth, No Place on Earth, The Faraway Country, The Curious Death of the Novel, The Wary Fugitives, The Writer in the South, The Teller in the Tale, George W. Cable, William Elliott Shoots a Bear, Virginia: A History, A Gallery of Southerners*, and *The Even-Tempered Angler*. He has been president of the Society for the Study of Southern Literature.

Elizabeth Spencer was born in Carrollton, Mississippi in 1921. She graduated from Belhaven College (B.A.) and Vanderbilt University (M.A.). She has taught at Ward-Belmont, Northwest Junior College, and Concordia University. She has been awarded fellowships by the National Institute of Arts and Letters and the Guggenheim Foundation. Her books include *Fire in the Morning, This Crooked Way, The Voice At the Back Door, Knights and Dragons, No Place for an Angel, Ship Island and Other Stories, The Snare, Collected Stories*, and *The Salt Line*. She lives with her husband, John A. B. Rusher, in Montreal, Quebec.

Max Steele was born in Greenville, South Carolina, in 1922. He attended Furman University and graduated from the University of North Carolina at Chapel Hill (1946). He studied at the Académie Julien and the Sorbonne, and was advisory editor to the *Paris Review*. He has taught at the University of California and since 1967 has been director of the creative writing program and professor of English at the University of North Carolina at Chapel Hill. His short stories have appeared in leading publications, and his books include a novel, *Debby*, which received both the Harper Prize and the Mayflower Award, *Where She Brushed Her Hair,* and *The Cat and the Coffee Drinkers.* He has received two O. Henry awards and a fellowship from the National Endowment for the Humanities.

Mark Smith is a native of Charlevoix, Michigan, attended school in Chicago, and graduated from Northwestern University. He has taught at the University of New Hampshire for many years, and lives in York Harbor, Maine. His novels include *Toyland, The Middleman, The Death of the Detective, The Moon Lamp,* and *The Delphinium Girl.* He has been awarded fellowships from the Guggenheim Foundation, the Rockefeller Foundation, the National Endowment for the Arts, and the Ingram Merrill Foundation.

Sylvia Wilkinson was born in Durham, North Carolina, in 1940. She studied with Randall Jarrell at the University of North Carolina at Greensboro (B.A.), with Howard Nemerov at Hollins College, and with Wallace Stegner at Stanford University. She has taught at the University of North Carolina at Asheville and at Chapel Hill, the College of William and Mary, the Learning Institute of North Carolina, Hollins College, Sweet Briar College, Washington University, and the University of Wisconsin–Milwaukee. Her books include *Moss on the North Side, A Killing Frost, Cale, The Stainless Steel Carrot, Shadow of the Mountain, Bone of My Bones,* and *Dirt Tracks to Glory,* as well as a number of children's books. She lives in El Segundo, California, and works as a timer at sports car and other automobile races throughout the United States and Europe, and as a correspondent for *Auto/Week.* She has received the Eugene Saxton Memorial Fellowship, the Wallace Stegner Fellowship, the Mademoiselle Merit Award, two Sir Walter Raleigh awards, and National Endowment for the Arts and Guggenheim fellowships.